The Work-Family Interface

For Phyllis Moen, who has taught me, and so many others, so much.

The Work-Family Interface

An Introduction

STEPHEN SWEET

Ithaca College

Los Angeles | London | New Delhi
Singapore | Washington DC

Los Angeles | London | New Delhi
Singapore | Washington DC

FOR INFORMATION:

SAGE Publications, Inc.
2455 Teller Road
Thousand Oaks, California 91320
E-mail: order@sagepub.com

SAGE Publications Ltd.
1 Oliver's Yard
55 City Road
London EC1Y 1SP
United Kingdom

SAGE Publications India Pvt. Ltd.
B 1/I 1 Mohan Cooperative Industrial Area
Mathura Road, New Delhi 110 044
India

SAGE Publications Asia-Pacific Pte. Ltd.
3 Church Street
#10-04 Samsung Hub
Singapore 049483

Acquisitions Editor: David Repetto
Editorial Assistant: Lauren Johnson
Production Editor: Brittany Bauhaus
Copy Editor: Mark Bast
Typesetter: C&M Digitals (P) Ltd.
Proofreader: Annie Lubinsky
Indexer: Diggs Publication Services, Inc.
Cover Designer: Janet Kiesel
Marketing Manager: Erica DeLuca
Permissions Editor: Karen Ehrmann

Copyright © 2014 by SAGE Publications, Inc.

Stephen Sweet has received permission to use all author photos shown in this text.

Printed in the United States of America

Library of Congress Cataloging-in-Publication Data

Sweet, Stephen A.

The work-family interface : an introduction / Stephen A. Sweet.

p. cm.—(Contemporary family perspectives)
Includes bibliographical references and index.

ISBN 978-1-4522-6878-1 (pbk. : alk. paper)

1. Work and family. 2. Work and family—United States. 3. Labor policy. 4. Family policy. I. Title.

HD4904.25.S94 2014
306.3'6—dc23   2012038265

This book is printed on acid-free paper.

13 14 15 16 17 10 9 8 7 6 5 4 3 2 1

Contents

Exhibits

Series Preface

Contemporary Family Perspectives

Susan J. Ferguson
Grinnell College

Stephen Sweet is an associate professor of sociology at Ithaca College and a visiting scholar at the Sloan Center on Aging & Work at Boston College. He has studied work and family issues for over 15 years, focusing on concerns such as the linked careers of dual earners, job insecurity, life course transitions, flexible work arrangements, productivity, and international variation in family supportive practices.

In this volume, *The Work–Family Interface: An Introduction,* Sweet argues that work and family institutions have the potential to be harmonized, but current arrangements commonly pit the interests of caregivers against those of employers (and visa versa). Compounding the problem is the intense commitment expected from caregivers and employees—roles commonly combined in the lives of contemporary workers. Throughout this book, Sweet illustrates how better understandings of work on the home front and work in the paid economy can be used to identify the sources of strains. These understandings are used to identify the most promising policies to address critical issues confronting workers, their families, their employers, and their communities.

The Work–Family Interface begins with an examination of the historical origins of contemporary dilemmas, showing how problems in the present result from predetermined cultural and institutional orientations. After providing this background, the next chapter reveals the diversity of work-family arrangements—focusing on a life course perspective that decenters analysis away from the archetypical traditional and dual-earner family arrangements. Sweet then reveals the strategies that families currently use to respond to work-family tensions and conflicts and the effect these paths have on lives and careers. The following chapter then looks at work-family tensions from the perspective of employers and how workplaces are responding to the needs of the changed workforce, such as by implementing flexible work schedules. Although this book focuses primarily on conditions in the United States, the fourth chapter shows the promise (as well as some not so positive implications) of following the approaches adopted in other countries. These international comparative analyses reveal that policy is largely determined by cultural values that sway collective responses to work-family tensions. The lessons learned elsewhere, as well as the increasing reliance on transnational production, indicate that effective harmonization of family requires establishing supports that enable families to provide and/or locate care. In addition, it requires establishing regulation within the work sphere—especially in respect to job security, work hours, and compensation. The final chapter concludes an assessment of the prospects for making work-family concerns a priority and suggests six national initiatives—advanced through the engagement of government—that can help reconcile work and family tensions.

A unique feature of this book is the use of original short-essay insights by 23 different family scholars. These insights, with accompanying photos of the authors, introduce the reader to diverse family scholars and their areas of study within the fields of work and family. The authors of these essays provide additional perspectives on work-family issues that enhance one's understanding of families in the United States and globally. Another unique feature of this volume is the mini projects located at the end of each chapter, which guide readers to apply the concepts they have learned.

The Work–Family Interface: An Introduction is appropriate for use in any class concerned with family structure, social inequality, and how employment affects families. Courses relating to human resource or talent management can also benefit from the book's careful consideration of the new workforce and the business case for flexible work. This book is a valuable resource to teachers and students in beginning and advanced courses in sociology, family studies, labor studies, women's studies, global studies, social work, public policy, and other disciplines. It also finds an audience among any person interested in comparative family studies or those who work in various human services fields, including human development, social work, education, counseling, health services, and the government. This last statement is particularly true for social service employees who work with families and other care workers. This volume can help them to better grasp the critical tensions that arise from the competing demands of families and employment.

Author Preface

A wealth of information exists on work and family concerns, revealing insights that were not present a few short decades ago. Compelling monographs provide rich ethnographic accounts of the challenges confronting specific groups of workers (i.e., contingent workers, flight attendants, women executives) and specific types of families (i.e., those entering retirement, young parents, those in poverty, those with children with special needs). Reports detail business-related concerns, such as how to make flexible work arrangements available and how to benchmark successes in managing work-family concerns. Social policies designed to ease work-family tensions—such as those that focus on family leave entitlements, access to childcare, and workplace protections—have been extensively studied. There are histories of change in the workplace and in the home, revealing the resonating effects that these changes have across institutions. Handbooks provide detailed treatment of concerns related to research, policy, and practice in the work-family field. And collections of resources—especially those provided through the online Work and Family Researchers Network (http://workfamily.sas.upenn.edu/)—enable one to locate a remarkable amount of information on specific concerns.

What is lacking, however, is a brief overview of the core concepts and issues central to the work-family area of inquiry, a primer that explains what "work-family" is and why work-family concerns are important to multiple stakeholders. This book intends to fill this gap by directing readers' attention to various ways of thinking about work-family connections and how these observations inform social policy. One concern is the variation in the ways work-family arrangements are configured and how perceptions of those configurations have shifted over time. Another concern is the way work affects family lives and how families strategically adapt to shifting opportunity structures and expectations. Equally important are the interests of employers, how they understand the impact of family on their operations, and how organizations are responding to the needs of a changed workforce. And as these concerns are identified, attention is directed to the interests of society itself and the policies and practices that shape lives on and off the job.

This book reveals the complex ways that work and family lives intersect, with a particular attention focused on employment and families in the United States, but as that country is compared and connected to other societies. By focusing on core concepts central to the different visions of the work-family interface, and by presenting issues to ponder, this book sets out to provide readers with the insights needed to locate work-family linkages. Beyond that, it is designed to provide guidance to help clarify stances on the best strategies to resolve concerns—not only as they exist in one's own complex life but also in the lives of others.

Acknowledgments

I thank series editor Susan Ferguson and David Repetto at Sage for inviting me to write this book, as well as for their helpful guidance. Judi Casey and Jerry Jacobs generously allowed me to use many definitions of work-family concepts as presented in the glossary of the Work and Family Researchers Network. I also greatly appreciate the willingness of leading scholars to compose brief summaries of their contributions to the field that are included in insight boxes throughout this book. These scholars include Anne Bardoel, Judi Casey, Kathleen Christensen, Shannon Davis, Laura den Dulk, Carla Freeman, Ellen Galinsky, Kathleen Gerson, Lonnie Golden, Janet Gornick, Joseph Grzywacz, Linda Haas, Brad Harrington, Jody Heymann, Erin Kelly, Ellen Ernst Kossek, Mila Lazarova, Phyllis Moen, Birgit Pfau-Effinger, Marcie Pitt-Catsouphes, Allison Pugh, Julie Rosenzweig, and Sarah Winslow. Bhavani Arabandi provided many helpful suggestions. Devon Ritz assisted in editing the manuscript, and Chelsea Russo assisted in composing graphic designs. Kevin Cahill, Suzanne Lawler, and Jacqueline James identified many promising practices of employers, as well as the logistical challenges of implementing these ways of working, and I am grateful that they allowed me to abstract some of their research. I also thank my students, who have helped me clarify strategies of explaining and presenting the ideas present in this book. Ithaca College generously granted me release time from teaching responsibilities, which greatly eased the process of writing. Data presented on flexible work arrangements and career insecurities originate from my earlier work at the Cornell Employment and Family Careers Institute and from my ongoing work at The Sloan Center on Aging & Work at Boston College, with support from the Alfred P. Sloan Foundation.

The author and SAGE would also like to acknowledge the contributions of the following reviewers:

Christopher Solario, *Chemeketa Community College*
David Maume, *University of Cincinnati*

Janet Puls, *Missouri Baptist University*
Melanie Deffendall, *Delgado Community College*
Michele Lee Kozimor-King, *Elizabethtown College*
Mirelle Cohen, *Olympic College*
Patricia E. Literte, *California State University, Fullerton*
Ryan Orr, *Millersville University*
Yvonne Vissing, *Salem State University*
Yvonne Moody, *Chadron State College*

And on the home front, a hearty thanks to my wife, Jai, for taking the lead while I worked early in the mornings and on weekends (but never at night!) and to our children, Arjun and Nisha, for being so fun and responsible.

Introduction

More than any other set of institutions, workplaces and families shape and give meaning to lives. While one intuitively knows that jobs affect family life, and family life affects work, American culture has ingrained the idea that work and family concerns are largely disconnected. For example, a person "goes to work" and "comes home to family." But on reflection, it is apparent that many problems experienced in the workplace can be directly traced to problems in the family. Or conversely, many problems experienced in the family can be directly traced to problems in the workplace. A few illustrations should more than suffice to illustrate some of the tensions.

- Becca is a single mother. She could be a dependable administrative assistant but is frequently absent or late to work because she cannot locate quality childcare that is affordable on her modest income. As a consequence, she relies on a combination of relatives and friends to watch her 3-year-old daughter Zoe.
- Charlene is a lawyer and has aspirations of becoming partner in her firm. She has been told (both directly and indirectly) that if she has children the prospects for achieving this goal are slim to nil.
- Jacob is 9 years old. He lives in a dangerous neighborhood and returns home to an empty house every day after school. He is expected to fix his own snack, do his homework, and help clean the house before his parents come home from their jobs. He is not allowed to have friends in the house alone.
- Imelda is a domestic worker living in Dubai, where she cleans and tends to the children of her employers. She has three young children that she has left behind in the Philippines in the care of her husband Tamir. She sends money home to her family and visits them usually once per year.
- Tom has been in a relationship with Keith for 10 years, but only a few of his coworkers know much about this dimension of his personal life. Keith has been diagnosed with terminal cancer, and Tom is so distracted by worry that his work is suffering. As a domestic partner, Keith is not included in Tom's employer-provided health insurance plan (which does cover married partners).

- Peter's aging mother lives 100 miles away from his home. During Peter's last visit, it became apparent that his mother needs personal assistance. Peter is going to need to take time away from his job in order to provide immediate care, as well as locate a suitable senior residential environment for her relocation. Because Peter has only worked for his employer for less than 3 months, he wonders what will happen when he requests this time off.

Concerns such as these are all too familiar, and it would be surprising if readers could not list numerous ways that their jobs (or those of their parents, children, or spouse) interfered with their family lives, or how their family lives have interfered with careers. And yet, all too often the hyphen that connects work to family, and family to work, is framed only in the negative, with a sole focus on institutional tensions. In many ways, because both institutions are so heavily reliant upon one another, each *contributes* to the other domain as well. Again, a few illustrations can establish the merits of this observation.

- Steve is a professor who gets great satisfaction from teaching students and engaging in research. He comes home with interesting stories to tell his wife and children (well, at least he thinks they are interesting).
- Jack and Susan operate a family business that has been remarkably successful. They now have a vacation home and ample resources to provide their children with many enriching activities.
- Doris and Jennifer met while working at the same company. They started first as coworkers, then as friends, then as lovers, and now as life partners. They are considering adopting a child.
- Brad, now retired, volunteers at a local elementary school. Even though he does not get paid, he considers this his "job" and takes great pleasure in helping children learn. He says, "This is my second act, the job I always wanted but never could have allowed myself to have."
- Silas and Karen have three children, one with special needs. Silas's job requires him to put in long hours, and Karen is the primary caretaker in the home. While not the life they had planned, Silas's career has flourished, in part, because Karen's work in the home has enabled him to devote himself to his job without distraction. They both believe this "traditional arrangement" has been best for their children.
- Michelle is an independent contractor who does copyediting for a publisher. Her job has lots of flexibility, and she is able to select how many projects she wishes to work on. During the winter months she takes on many projects so that during the summer she can work less and visit her sister (who lives three states away). During these visits, she takes care of her sister's children while her sister continues to work in a job that does not offer this type of flexibility.

As these cases illustrate, work can be a source of rewards that are essential to family success. Work enhances people's social networks, makes them interesting, and integrates them into activities that are often vital to the maintenance and reproduction of society. The same can be said of family and what it does for the capacity to work.

Those lucky to have ideal family situations and ideal jobs arguably "have it all." And yet even when one has what he or she hopes for in the home and in the workplace, sometimes the two institutions chafe against one another. Both the workplace and the family are "greedy institutions" and expect intense and undivided commitment (Coser, 1974). While maybe manageable in one domain or the other, the combined demands that each institution places on people can be unbearably heavy. The weights of these burdens are influenced not only by the amount of effort involved, but also by how tasks are synchronized. And social processes place unequal strains on the basis of gender and life stage. The results are binds that can force hard choices to select family over career, career over family, or perhaps other sacrifices such as job and family over community involvement or personal interests (Hochschild, 1997; Moen & Roehling, 2005; Stone, 2007).

What are the consequences of these hard choices? As discussed in the chapters that follow, for workers outcomes can be diminished health, financial hardship, career compromise, ambivalence, and dissatisfaction. For their spouses, children, parents, and neighbors, the outcomes of these choices can create absences that affect the quality of support received and even threaten family stability. For employers, outcomes can result in undependable and distracted workers, as well as undermine the capacity to recruit, retain, and develop talent. And for society writ large, these outcomes can limit collective attachments to work and family such that reproductive rates fall, marginalized members are left without care, and social inequalities are exacerbated. Ultimately the hope is for work-family arrangements that do not require hard choices. Achieving this objective requires not only understanding the social structures that define the arenas in which work and family roles are performed, but also the cultural templates—the deeply embraced values and beliefs—that shape personal and societal expectations.

To illuminate the concerns of multiple stakeholders, the chapters that follow focus on different ways of understanding work-family connections, different types of structural arrangements, and the implications for workers, their families, their employers, and their societies. The goal is not to provide an exhaustive overview of the many concerns identified, but rather to highlight the existence of the work-family interface and implications of different ways of thinking about, or structuring, that interface. Within each chapter, readers will find contributions composed by leading scholars in the work-family field, describing the implications of their major insights. In addition to referenced definitions of important work and family concepts, the book concludes with direction on how to find more information on relevant work and family scholarship, policy, and practice. Throughout, readers will learn of concepts and perspectives central to work-family scholarship and policy analysis. Each chapter concludes with a mini project, an activity that can be performed in a short amount of time to further illuminate how work-family connections may relate to one's own life and perspectives.

One of the most important contributions of work-family scholarship is a reconsideration of taken-for-granted cultural and structural configurations, addressing the question of "how did the current arrangements emerge?" Chapter 1 considers work-family configurations from a historical perspective, identifying how many current concerns resulted from shifts in the culture and structure of society over time. Suggested in the chapter is that in society today most everyone is expected to work. And yet, policies and expectations remain grounded in old (and sometimes flawed) ways of connecting work and family. The result is that many current work-family arrangements rub against outdated institutional practices and expectations. This leads to the insight that contemporary work-family concerns originate as a consequence of structural and cultural lags, or of enduring failures to recognize the limitations of institutionalized practices.

Who is the typical worker, and what is the typical family? Answering this question presents numerous challenges, as contemporary workforces and households are remarkably variable. And yet, having some sense of the lives of particular classes of workers and families is a central concern in identifying both the challenges present today and the most promising means of addressing those challenges. Chapter 2 considers the constellations of work-family arrangements present among different members of society. Drawing attention to how the needs and capacities to work and provide care fluctuate throughout the life course, the importance of addressing diversity is shown as an essential strategy in reconciling work and family tensions. Because the world is not "one size fits all" (and few would wish for such an arrangement) this requires policies and practices that enable people to fit work and family in customizable arrangements.

How are workers responding to work-family tensions in their lives? To answer this question, Chapter 3 turns to the issue of personal and family adaptive strategies, the ways that people respond to work-family tensions and the consequences for life quality. This chapter focuses on concerns of agency, the ways that people make tough choices and the consequences these choices have on their lives. On the one hand, this chapter affirms the remarkable resilience of working families and that even when tensions are considerable, so are the creative responses to resolving these strains. On the other hand, many of the responses result in less than happy trade-offs. Revealing the cost associated with work-family conflict—especially as incurred on the family front—is critical to identifying what needs to change.

Work-family tensions not only negatively affect families, they also undermine business success. To identify the magnitude of these implications, Chapter 4 focuses on the employer side of the work-family equation, considering the reasons why employers should consider their workers' family concerns when designing jobs and work expectations. When employers adopt promising practices, such as advancing flexible work arrangements, it has the potential to create positive returns such as increased employee commitment. However, there are reasons why many employers are not attentive to their employees' lives off the job, leading to a conclusion that self-interest may guide some employers to reconsider job designs, but it will not necessarily guide all workplaces to become family friendly.

The globalization of work presents even further challenges, as it operates (to a considerable extent) beyond the confines of what any individual nation state might dictate. Adding to the complexity are huge variations in both the quality of work opportunities in any locale and the expectations of workers themselves. Chapter 5 focuses on the issue of cross-national variation in work-family contexts, as well as the impact that transnational trade, labor flows, and production have on the work-family interface. As industries and workers themselves move across national boundaries, increased complexities are emerging in the establishment of a global economy that is truly family friendly. While globalization may ease work-family strains in some societies, it can paradoxically do this by exacerbating strains in other societies. When work and family concerns are understood solely as domestic issues, the implications for those who move to find work, or who labor for absentee employers, remain hidden from policy initiatives.

The final chapter considers societal objectives in addressing discord in the work-family interface, as informed by observations that family adaptation and business adaptation are going to have, at best, only partial success in advancing harmonization. Chapter 6 identifies the role governments can play in structuring the arena in which work and family interact. Proactive government engagement in work regulation, incentivizing behaviors, provision of resources, and other directives can positively affect the capacities to engage in work and to provide care. However, policies intersect with culture in complex ways, such that no single society can be demonstrated as having "figured out" how to reconcile work and family tensions. The question left to readers is what type of society they wish the United States to be, and the text challenges them to frame their perspective in respect to what has been demonstrated as achievable (but not without costs) elsewhere.

This book is written primarily to help Americans understand what they should expect from themselves, their families, their employers, and their society. It also is intended to help clarify personal roles in moving society in directions that hold the greatest promise. For these reasons, the focal point of the work-family interface is the United States. This is not to move attention away from the needs of workers and families in other societies. I offer no pretense that answers to any of the concerns presented are easily resolved, but they certainly can be resolved much more effectively than they currently are. Finding the paths will require trade-offs, compromise on the part of both workers and employers, and a rebalancing of commitment to collective interests. But above all, it will require an openness to see what needs to be changed, the knowledge to know what has the potential to work, and the political will to move change forward. This book is written to help advance those objectives.

1

Origins of Contemporary Work-Family Dilemmas

It is self-evident that work today is performed in ways very different from earlier periods. Few people tend to crops, milk cows, or make their own cheese. And yet new ways of working are reopening opportunities to return to old ways of integrating work and family. For example, the modern technologies that make telecommuting possible enable work to be performed in and around the home, much in the way that work was performed in and around the home in agrarian societies. So although few workers today are engaged in family farming, it is possible for many workers to perform their jobs while also tending to soup simmering on the stove and children at their feet. But one wonders, how familiar would society's predecessors find the experiences and expectations of these modern work-at-home families? Would the sources of satisfaction and frustration with the work-family interface be similar? This first chapter looks to the past to consider the origins of some major contemporary work-family concerns.

This chapter discusses not only the technological and organizational changes that make work today different from the arrangements of the preceding decades and centuries, but also the profound cultural changes that accompanied the transformation of workplaces and families. Because of these changes, even when opportunities to redesign work or family arrangements are present, it can be difficult to do so because what one expects of (and from) a job and of (and from) a family is to a great extent rooted in the past. Fundamental preexisting templates—such as understandings of what is (and is not) work, job structures, and real and believed boundaries that separate lives at home from those on the job—confront working families today and constrain their options.

To illuminate these concerns the focus is on the historical transformation of work-family relations and the shift from household economies to present-day arrangements in which nearly everyone is expected to work. The primary intent here is to identify changes in the ways workplaces and families *are connected,* as well as changes in the *ways ideal arrangements are culturally defined.*

When Work Separated From Family: The Household Economy Transitions to the Industrial Economy

For most of human history, work and family institutions overlapped to such a great extent that these domains were inextricably intertwined in the day-to-day lives of people. Rather than "work" or "family" there was, more or less, simply "life." Even if one traces work-family relations back only a few hundred years, to a time when most families operated on the basis of household economies, work and family were pushed together in intimate ways. Because nearly all economic activity occurred in and around the home, family members did not "go to work" nor did they "come home." But beyond this observation, it is important to also understand that tasks that later came to be viewed as "not work" (activities such as household maintenance, cooking, and childcare) were understood as essential contributions to the family economy (Boris & Lewis, 2006).

Today there is a tendency to consider the family domain as the place of consumption, the area in a person's life that absorbs economic resources. People work in order to provide income for their families. Work, on the other hand, is the place of production and the place where people contribute to society by expanding economic wealth. And we engage in considerable boundary work to establish different identities and purposes in each domain (Desrochers, 2003; Nippert-Eng, 1996). For example, people wear different clothes in the home and in the workplace, focus attention on how far they let work intrude into their lives, and contemplate how intimate they should allow themselves to be with coworkers.

In Colonial America (and prior) the division between home and work was not so clear-cut. For example, slave families were treated and defined by their Southern owners as a means to create wealth. But the practice of slavery was not the only way work-family structures were explicitly economic in practice and social definition. In the Northern colonies, it was common for families to take in live-in boarders to assist in the production of goods used for barter or sale. Within the household economy, food and shelter were a part of the compensation received, and in that context the labor involved in keeping a good home had tangible economic consequences. And in addition to live-in boarders, children also were collectively defined as a means to secure labor. Parents understood their children not as precious little crea-tures but more as miniature adults with a responsibility to contribute to the family economy (not just receive from it). Even in the early stages of indus-trialization, children brought more income to household economies than did wives (Gratton & Moen, 2004, 2007).

In the 18th century, gender roles were well established, but there also was considerable overlap between the duties and responsibilities of wives and husbands, which enhanced recognition of the economic value of the labor women provided. For example, if a husband lost his capacity to work, the wife (a man's "help meet") could assume the role of "deputy husband" and control business affairs until he was able to return to work (Ulrich, 1982). In other words, while a wife's place might have been primarily in the home, it was not solely restricted to that domain, and she could move beyond it when the family needed. Women also managed workers employed in the household economy and historical records indicate that they could be "wisely awful" to their charges if work did not meet their expectations. Frailty, which came to be viewed as a feminine virtue in the 19th century, had no place in a system that required wives to perform hard physical work. But beyond sometimes engaging in comparable work, because husbands and wives mutually wit-nessed each other's efforts, it promoted a sense of shared respect that the maintenance of the home involved *real work*. Historical analyses reveal with certainty that, prior to industrialization, reproduction and care work were understood as contributing to the family economy, not (as it was later to be culturally defined) as absorbing economic resources (Crittenden, 2001).

Finally, consider that the temporal spaces that separated work and family labor were not rigidly structured and had a much weaker relation to chrono-logical time. For example, most people did not commute from work to home or from home to work. As a consequence, the boundaries between work and family tasks were far more fluid than the way they are today. If crops needed to be harvested, all family members could be called to work in the field. If the merchant capitalist was coming for his order, husbands, wives, children, and boarders might labor late into the night. And if it was winter, and there was little work to be done, one could relax (but also cook, clean, and provide care). So not only were work and family roles understood differently than they are today, they also were organized and paced differently (Thompson, 1967). What all this shows is that the notion of coming home from work or exiting the home to work is a modern cultural construction.

One should be hesitant to view work-family relations as they existed in Colonial America as "the good old days." Lives were short, division of labor was uneven, multiple forms of abuse and exploitation were present, workplace protections were nonexistent, and supports for families rested almost entirely on kin networks and local charity. However, by looking back, one can see that the organization of work and family relations, as well as the cultural mind-set about how these two institutions are connected, were very different as compared to today's taken-for-granted arrangements and understandings. Some would go so far as to argue that the integration of work and family within the household economy was a more natural way of arranging lives. After all, work being performed in and around the home was the normative arrangement up until the industrial revolution, pitting thousands of years of human history against the past two centuries. The desire to meld work and family together might explain why many workers today seek greater flexibility in their work arrangements, such that they might be able to bring their work home, or even their families to work. However, not everyone shares those preferences, as cultural values in the wake of the industrial revolution shifted to emphasize the advantages of separating family from work.

The onset of the industrial revolution (which occurred roughly from 1790 to 1830) is commonly attributed to the creation of inventions such as the spinning jenny (which enabled the twining of multiple spools of thread at the same time) and the harnessing of water power (which unleashed the potentials of wide-scale mechanization of production). Factories that combined consistent sources of energy with mass production technologies were able to produce goods at a much higher volume and (when successful) at a much greater profit than was possible under the putting-out system of the household economy. But it was not simply technology that made this possible; it also was the reorganization of work and family institutions to correspond with new temporal arrangements.

Today most employees labor according to schedules that specify when they are to appear at work and when they can leave. While the organization of work according to time rather than task is now a widely accepted (but also increasingly challenged) practice, this was not the case in the early 19th century. The 40-hour work week, weekends, and vacations emerged as products of negotiation and conflict between workers and employers on the terms of labor (Rybczynski, 1991). New standards of conduct also were negotiated, as tardiness and absenteeism were rampant in the early stages of industrialization, leading to systems of enforcing schedule compliance. While workers were accustomed to working on an "as needed" basis in the household economy and continued to assert autonomy on the timing at which work took place, employers lamented that too much honor was given to Saint Monday (the patron saint of the weekend hangover). As the culture attempted to come to terms with what constituted a fair day's wage for a fair day's work, new concerns emerged such as whether workers should receive pay if they failed to show up to work for reasons such as sickness or if they should be paid extra after laboring longer hours.

While today industrialization is heralded as a milestone in human history, at the time members of the working class did not view it as a positive step forward—in part because of the impact it had on their ways of organizing family lives. The new industrial order not only created new "work time" arrangements, it also reconfigured "family time" arrangements. For example, the advent of shift work, which required employees to move into and out of work at rigidly defined times, created new sets of tensions in the management of household affairs, as these shifts created absences that undermined the capacity of families to provide care (Hareven, 1982). And in contrast to the household economy, because industrial capitalism curtailed family economic self-sufficiency, the prospect of unemployment presented a looming threat that shaped many aspects of life. For example, workers understood that the reputation of their relatives affected the prospects of receiving employment and that one's own conduct could result in retaliation against other family members. As parents, spouses, and siblings commonly worked within the same factory walls, and because retribution could be meted out by vindictive supervisors, consequences could be severe (Jacoby, 1991). For these reasons, the intimate connection between work and the family comprised a means by which employers exerted control over their workforces. However, family loyalties also were critical components of the labor movement, as family members could attract and pressure relatives to join unions.

In the early stages of industrialization, employers constructed their operations with a tacit understanding that work was connected to family. Consider that in the 19th century the Amoskaeg textile factory in New Hampshire (at the time the world's largest textile manufacturer) provided workers with subsidized housing, social activities, recreational resources, profit-sharing options, a retirement program, an employee welfare program, English classes, access to nursing services, charity to widows, an accident ward, dental care for children, and playgrounds. While no doubt these resources created incentives to not seek employment elsewhere, it is noteworthy that the Amoskaeg company was not legally required to provide these services, nor were the resources the product of collective negotiation from organized labor. It is hard not to conclude that the company adopted paternalistic practices because it viewed caring for employees *and their families* as a social obligation (Hareven & Langenbach, 1978).

In sum, prior to industrialization, work and family were intimately connected both physically and ideologically. With industrialization, a greater physical separation between work and the home was introduced, and some ideological elements began to shift as well. However, families continued to be integrated into the workplace as collectivities (i.e., kin working with kin). Lines between work and family were being drawn, but they were not as tightly configured as they were to become in the 20th century. And as discussed shortly, these new boundaries not only separated work from home, they also built walls between women's careers and men's, and they diminished the stature and economic valuation of household labor.

When Family and Work Were Defined as Separate Spheres: The Husband/Breadwinner–Wife/Homemaker Economy

During the 20th century, a new work-family configuration emerged, assigning the duty of economic provision to the husband and the maintenance of home and children to the wife. This arrangement did not solidify overnight, as it involved a gradual renegotiation of gender role assignments, as well as other expectations such as the reconsideration of children as "precious objects." By the mid-1920s, this husband/breadwinner–wife/homemaker ideal had largely defined employer practices and the very limited public policies that existed at the time (Boris & Lewis, 2006). For example, it was considered acceptable (and in society's best interests) for employers to terminate a woman's employment once she had children. But the expectation did not remain consistent throughout the 20th century, as women were temporarily integrated into the paid labor force during World War II and into jobs that had been performed almost exclusively by men. And as noted by social historians, even when this husband/breadwinner–wife/homemaker arrangement was at its cultural peak in the 1950s, numerous families were excluded from this ideal—most notably low-income African American women, who were integrated as domestic workers employed by middle- and upper-class white households (Coontz, 2000; Nakano Glenn, 2002). Nonetheless, the husband/breadwinner–wife/homemaker model was presented in popular culture, academic research, and legal framework as an ideal design, one that should be used to measure one's own family against and one that should be socially reinforced. And even for those who could not live up to this expectation, many presented fronts suggesting that they were conforming to this template. For example, lower-income immigrant women kept much of their work hidden by performing piecework in the home rather than seeking outside employment.

The ever-present adoring wife and mother became a cultural mainstay of the 20th century. The home was to be a haven in a heartless world, the domain where husbands could recover from the cold instrumental relations of the factory or corporate world (Lasch, 1995). The difficulties that this arrangement placed on family lives—especially for women—were not culturally acknowledged, leading the pioneering feminist Betty Friedan (1963) in *The Feminine Mystique* to label these strains as "the problem that has no name." Women who failed to live up to these ideals, or who did not feel a sense of emotional satisfaction while attempting to do so, were viewed as having personal failings. In response to these stresses, at midcentury the dominant culture focused on strategies for making families function not by examining institutional arrangements, but rather by focusing on personal behavior. If families were unstable or lacking in sexual satisfaction, happiness, or emotional gratification, the problem rested in the home front. The popular press, academic researchers, pop psychologists, and others offered advice and guidance on the best ways of saving marriages and the institution itself (Celello, 2009). Until the feminist movement of the 1960s took hold, scant attention focused on the dark side of the ideals presented on shows such as *Ozzie & Harriet* or *Leave it to Beaver,* which affirmed the notions of privatized families, who neither needed or demanded resources beyond those that could be secured by two spouses fulfilling their separate gender roles inside and outside the home.

During the 20th century, the gender division of work and home resulted in many men and women inhabiting separate social spheres with distinct gender role scripts. Beyond the reality of separate spheres, the culture also embraced values in support of gendered divisions of labor inside and outside the home, especially the idea that work and family are not connected, except to the extent that work was a means to provide for family. Largely unacknowledged by the culture were the ways families provided economic contributions by reproducing, nurturing, and socializing the next generation of workers or by providing services off the job to the current generation of (male) workers.

The critique of the ideology of separate spheres—that the successes of employers inherently involve the provision of services by families—has been one of the most important contributions of work-family research for the past three decades. But the extent that this observation has translated into concrete policy changes has been limited. Entertain for a moment the idea that corporations and entire societies are reliant on the work that is performed in the home in order to secure the next generation of worker/citizens. If that is true, then why shouldn't people be compensated for the work that they perform in the home? In other words, should one be paid to mother? And if so, how much should the compensation be? The friction that this notion presents is a product of the ideology of separate spheres, because the act of mothering is considered to be noneconomic, and when it is considered in respect to economic consequences, it is commonly viewed as *absorbing* resources rather than creating them. And for many, the idea of paying family caregivers profanes the sacred rewards that are received from assisting children, aging parents, or broader kin networks. This work is above financial compensation, says the ideology of separate spheres (Crittenden, 2001).

While policies will be discussed in more detail later, consider a couple of the consequences of viewing mothering (or caregiving to other kin) as an economically nonproductive act. Families incur numerous economic penalties for having children, as the vast majority of resources given to children are expected to be privately provided. Children are very expensive. The U.S. Department of Agriculture (Lino, 2012) estimates that for a middle-income household the cost of raising a child in 2011 to the age of 18 was $268,884.

While most Americans believe that a child is best served by having a close attachment to a mother in early childhood, there are few economic rewards for engaging in this behavior, as paid family leave options are unavailable to most American workers. The fact that a transition into parenthood is among the strongest predictors of a transition into poverty is truly disheartening. One solution to this problem would be to extend economic resources to those engaged in parenting, but so long as parenting is considered a noneconomic activity, there is little hope of advancing such a proposition.

Even further, consider current welfare policy in the United States. In order to receive cash assistance under the Temporary Assistance to Needy Families program, single parents are expected to engage in work outside of the home. This work requirement was instituted in 1996, under the Personal Responsibility and Work Opportunity Reconciliation Act, in an effort to move welfare recipients into the labor force. In part, this legislation was motivated by the message advanced by some conservative groups, casting poor stay-at-home mothers as "welfare queens" and part of an "underclass" that perpetuated a cultural acceptance of welfare dependency as a way of life (Murray, 1995). Key to the logic of advancing a work requirement for welfare receipt was the assumption that the work that poor women perform in service of their own children (as well as in service of broader kin networks) had little social value. In response, the new policy pushed "responsibility" in a manner that left many children unattended or in poorly supervised care situations as their parents entered into low-paying dead-end jobs. One must question the idea that the immediate circumstances of children, and their futures, are better off as a consequence of the proposition that work performed in and around the home absorbs social resources rather than contributes to societal wealth (Crouter & Booth, 2004).

On the work front, the wife/homemaker role had a major impact on job designs, and again, this legacy remains. The work-family ideals of the 20th century "freed" husbands to be undistracted by home affairs. As a consequence employers could expect (and often demand) that their workers labor long hours. Workers could be told to stay late at a last-minute's notice or travel if the job demanded it. To move up in the corporate world, intense commitment was expected, and the employees whose cars were first in the parking lots and the last to leave were rewarded with promotions and increased security. These expectations are now hardwired into job codes. For example, American employers are entitled to terminate employees who refuse to work overtime, senior-level positions are restricted to those who are willing to put in intense effort, and "mommy track" jobs are largely dead-end assignments. Today's ideal worker is yesterday's male employee. The problem is one of structural lag, that many women and men not only no longer desire these career arrangements, they also cannot fulfill these expectations without remarkable costs to their families (Williams, 2000).

Making Up the Rules About Life's Jobs

Marcie Pitt-Catsouphes

At the Center on Aging and Work, my colleagues and I have focused a lens on the multigenerational workforce and the ways age maps onto the concerns of workers, their families, and their employers. Consider that in the 1970s today's older workers were yesterday's younger workers, pioneering new strategies and cultural standards. As a consequence, younger single parents today feel far less stigmatized at work and in the community than they did a few decades ago. Likewise, dual-earner couples today are far less likely to consider themselves selfish for enjoying their careers. The common theme expressed by these early work-family pioneers was the feeling that they were operating without any script; they had to make up the rules (and create their own resources) almost every day.

As they progress into their later career stages, today's older workers are pioneering new narratives of work and family connections. They are extending labor force participation past the time of traditional retirement. Whereas the concept of "working in retirement" was an oxymoron just a short time age, older adults are redefining options for post-late-career employment. These options might include reduced-hours arrangements (sometimes in a phased retirement structure), contract work, or some form of entrepreneurship. And, of course, their families have changed over the years. Approximately 4 of every 10 workers in the United States reports that they have provided care to a loved one over the age of 65 in the previous 5 years. With increased longevity, experts predict that the numbers and percentages of working caregivers will continue to increase.

The challenge continues to be one of mismatch. If the baby boomer work-family pioneers are to leave a legacy for their children and grandchildren, may it be expressed by widespread adoption of more flexible work structures that can leverage worker engagement while celebrating the importance of rich personal and family lives across the life course.

Marcie Pitt-Catsouphes directs the Sloan Center on Aging & Work at Boston College where she is on faculty at the Graduate School of Social Work and the Carroll School of Management. She recently coauthored a chapter, "Optimizing the Long Future of Aging: Beyond Involvement to Engagement," that will appear in the *Handbook on Aging, Work and Society* (Sage, in press).

Family-Work Relationship in Cultural and Institutional Context

Birgit Pfau-Effinger

Two decades ago I sought explanations for why the majority of women (or parents) in different countries behave differently in relation to their labor force participation, part-time work, and organization of childcare. I developed the theoretical approach of the "gender arrangement" as an overall explanation for such differences: the interaction of cultural, institutional, social, structural, and economic factors, as well as actors' constellations, in the societal context. It defines "culture" as the collective set of values, models, and belief systems in a society, conceptualized here as the "gender culture" based on dominant or marginalized cultural family models in a society. The gender arrangement and gender culture can be contradictory, contested, and changeable.

I used this theoretical approach for different cross-sectional and historical analyses. It emerged that the majority of women in each country relate their employment and childcare behavior to a specific set of cultural family values about "motherhood," "childhood," and the "family-employment" relationship. Family policies and economic factors can support or hinder their realization. In several comparative historical analyses I show how the development of women's employment and childcare behavior in European gender arrangements since the mid-20th century took different paths, which can mainly be explained by deep-rooted historical differences in the gender culture. Such differences in historical development paths in the gender culture also help explain why in their behavior regarding employment vis-à-vis childcare, women with young children in eastern Germany still use the options of the welfare state's policy in a different manner than mothers in western Germany.

Wanting also to explain why the strength of the cultural model of the male-breadwinner family differed in European societies in the mid-20th century, I showed that historically the positioning and power of the urban bourgeoisie in these different societies is important, since this class was the "social carrier" of this cultural family model.

Birgit Pfau-Effinger is full professor of sociology and director, Centre for Globalisation and Governance, Faculty of Social Sciences, at the University of Hamburg, Germany, publishes extensively on the family-employment relationship, and is coauthor of "Differences in Women's Employment Patterns and Family Policies: Eastern and Western Germany" in *Community, Work & Family* 14, 2:217–32 (2011).

Where We Are Now: Most Every Adult Should Work Outside the Home

As the 20th century drew to a close, expectations about what families should be, and how they should connect to work, shifted. There is a far greater acceptance of a diversity of family forms, which include not only same-sex relationships, but also single-parent families and childless families (all of which were heartily discouraged in the husband/bread-winner–wife/homemaker model). In addition, proximate to the early 1970s, shifting expectations and economic needs compelled large proportions of women to enter the paid labor force. This dual-earner arrangement has been identified by some as "the new normal" (Boris & Lewis, 2006).

Exhibit 1.1 shows that women's participation in the paid labor force has doubled since 1940, and today the proportion of women working nearly matches that of men. Exhibit 1.2 shows the impact of this trend on family-work configurations as they are identified among married couples. Most married couples in the United States, irrespective of whether they have children or not, have both spouses employed outside of the home, and these families include couples that have young children as well.

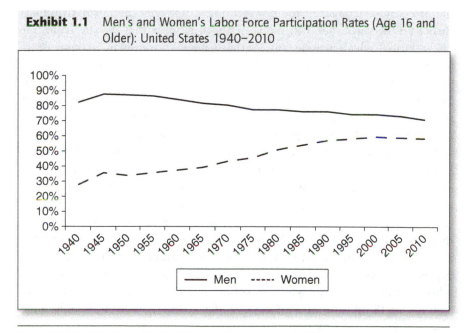

Exhibit 1.1   Men's and Women's Labor Force Participation Rates (Age 16 and Older): United States 1940–2010

Sources: Historical Abstracts of the United States, Bureau of Labor Statistics

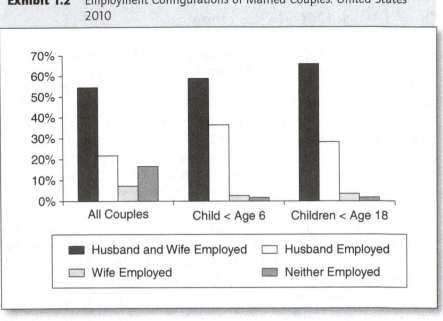

Exhibit 1.2 Employment Configurations of Married Couples: United States 2010

Sources: Statistical Abstracts of the United States

The next chapter considers in more detail why it is important to appreciate the diversity of families in the new economy, not only the normative dual-earner arrangement, but also the varieties of families that deviate from this "new norm," which include couples that follow "traditional" arrangements (approximately one in three couples), and how extended-kin relationships shape the ways work and family are integrated. And throughout subsequent discussion, attention is drawn to other forms of diversity (such as those that relate to sexual orientation, social class positioning, disability) as also influencing the work-family interface. Here are two observations.

First, the arrangements constructed in the 20th-century breadwinner/ homemaker economy chafe in a society where the expectation is that most every adult should work. While employees are expected to perform according to the standards of the ideal worker (show up on time, work long hours), their lives off the job provide far less support. And as larger proportions of the population enter the paid labor force, far fewer hours are now available to perform the support duties in neighborhoods and communities. Locating people who have the time and energy to be Boy Scout or Girl Scout leaders, who can run the PTA, or who can volunteer at hospice becomes ever more challenging (Bookman, 2004; Gerstel & Sarkesian, 2006). And while there is less time to devote to the community, the intensity of energies is focused ever more tightly on two concerns: careers and families, as there is little time for anything else.

A second observation is that few social institutions have made many meaningful changes that sufficiently address new work-family institutional arrangements and strains. For example, schools operate in accordance with schedules established in the 19th-century agrarian economy, providing instruction to students for an average of 180 days per year. That leaves 80 weekdays in which working parents need to locate alternate care arrangements for their children. Childcare and eldercare service options are lacking in most communities, and among those that exist, quality arrangements are unaffordable to many families. Parents are expected to maintain careers but also to be present with their children (especially at young ages), and few options make this possible. And as seen in subsequent chapters, the provision of flexible work arrangements (which have the potential to facilitate work-family integration) remains limited and unevenly allocated. These structural and cultural lags indicate a 21st-century economy that operates on the basis of 20th-century (and sometimes 19th-century) institutional arrangements.

Summary

The definitions of "normal" or "traditional" work and family arrangements have shifted over time. At each juncture of change in the work world, family ideals changed as well. While work-family researchers understand (but less so the general public) that the labor performed in the home has tremendous economic value, society has yet to institutionalize means of rewarding this work for the value it creates. Today an economy in which most every adult is expected to labor outside of the home is the norm. And yet, the way people think about how work is to be performed is informed by codes of conduct established when one in two adult family members was not scripted to work. Addressing these concerns requires not only reconsidering *how* people perform work and family duties, but also the *expectations* for labor as it occurs in both domains.

Useful Concepts

Boundary work. "The process through which we organize potentially realm-specific matters, people, objects, and aspects of self into 'home' and 'work,' maintaining and changing these conceptualizations as needed and/or desired" (Nippert-Eng, 1996, pp. 7–8).

Care work. "The work of caring for others, including unpaid care for family members and friends, as well as paid care for others. Caring work includes taking care of children, the elderly, the sick, and the disabled, as well as doing domestic work such as cleaning and cooking. As reproductive labor, care work is necessary to the continuation of every society. By deploying the term 'care work,' scholars and advocates emphasize the importance of recognizing that care is not simply a natural and uncomplicated response to those in need, but actually hard physical, mental, and emotional work, which is often unequally distributed through society (Meyer, 2000). Because care tends to be economically devalued, many scholars who study care work emphasize the skill required for care, and the importance of valuing care" (Misra, 2007).

Dual-earner families. "Marriages in which both partners pursue occupational careers" (Marshall, 2003).

Greedy institutions. Institutions that require intense commitment and loyalty. Membership within greedy institutions is often contingent on the capacity to extend remarkable effort and dedication to others within that institution and its goals. The family and the workplace are both greedy institutions in most people's lives (Coser, 1974).

Household economy. "Under this system, all the inhabitants of an individual household—husband, wife, children, servants, or slaves, extended kin, and other boarders—labored together to produce the goods necessary for the household maintenance. The sites of work and home overlapped, so much so that they were virtually indistinguishable from one another. So too, was women's reproductive and productive labor" (Boris & Lewis, 2006, p. 75).

Ideal worker. "The ideal worker is someone who works at least forty hours a week year round. This ideal-worker norm, framed around the traditional life patterns of men, excludes most mothers of childbearing age" (Williams, 2000, p. 2).

Ideology of separate spheres. The belief that work and family institutions have few connections, the terms of employment have little or no impact on family lives, and the work performed within the family domain has little relation to workplace functioning (Beggren, 2010).

Industrial welfare. Arrangements in which employers voluntarily provide services to employees beyond base wages. These services can take myriad forms, and many are intended to help enhance employees' and their family members' lives off the job. Industrial welfare also is called corporate paternalism (Hareven & Langenbach, 1978).

Traditional family. "The concept of the traditional family, that is, the 'natural reproductive unit' of mom, pop, and the children all living under one roof, is not an immutable one. It is a social construct that varies from culture to culture and, over time, the definition changes within a culture" (Ball, 2002, p. 68).

Issues to Ponder

1. Suppose that you could be "hired" to take the place of a parent of a 2-year-old child for 1 year. During that year you get to do all of the good things with that child (play with him or her, tuck the child in at bedtime) but also all of the drudgery (laundry, cleaning, being available and attentive at nearly all moments). How much would someone have to pay you to take this job that involves your devoted commitment nearly 24 hours a day, 7 days a week, for an entire year? Whatever figure you arrive at, can you explain why the "real parent" of that child should not receive similar compensation?

2. Suppose you had the opportunity for both you and your spouse (or the spouse you might have in the future) to work in your home for the same enterprise. You share a home office, your work tasks overlap, and you spend most of your day in her or his company. Would this approximation of the household economy be your ideal work-family arrangement? If not, what would be? What would be the upside and downside to coworking situations such as this?

3. For the sake of argument, accept the premise that every able-bodied adult member of society should be expected to work outside of the home. If such a deal is struck, in reciprocity what should these workers be entitled to expect from their employers and their society? Consider issues such as pay standards, schedule standards, opportunities for growth, job security, and childcare and elder care resources. To what extent is this other side of the deal being satisfied?

4. Today the ideal worker is modeled on the script established for men in the mid-20th century. This involves working long hours, uninterrupted and without distraction. Brief vacations are accepted but not prolonged breaks, and work comes before family. In a society where everyone is expected to work, suppose all members strive to live up to this ideal. What are the consequences for individuals, families, employers, and communities?

5. If you were to redefine the behavior standards applied to the ideal worker of the 21st century—keeping in mind concerns of parents who attend school functions, adult children who provide care for aging parents, women who give birth, men who adopt children—what should those standards be? Consider concerns such as the number of hours expected of that ideal worker (45? 40? 35? 30?), attendance records (always on time?), and breaks (Rights to a vacation and or family leave?).

Mini Project

Place a call to a friend or family relation from your parents' and/or grand-parents' generation. Ask that person to talk about his or her work-family experiences and the attitudes that were present when he or she was in early adulthood. Some questions you might ask follow.

- o When you were a young adult, what were your career aspirations?
- o When you were a young adult, what were your aspirations for your family?
- o As your family commitments developed, did that affect your career? How?
- o Did your career affect your family commitments? How?
- o What changes have you seen in the ways members of my generation approach their families as compared to your generation?
- o What changes have you seen in the ways members of my generation approach their work and careers as compared to your generation?

Compare their perspectives with your anticipated life course and past experiences.

2

Diversity of Work, Family, and Work-Family Arrangements

If one were able to take a snapshot of every person in society, nearly endless combinations of work, family, and work-family arrangements would show up. These include workers with great jobs but whose marriages are falling apart; workers who have terrible jobs but whose families affirm their personal worth; those who are work rich and family rich, receiving many rewards in both domains; those who are work poor and family poor, receiving few rewards in either domain; and on and on. If one were to make a movie of every person in society, movement into and out of different configurations through the life course would become apparent. For example, a happily married couple might separate, and a job holder might retire. And if given omniscience and the ability to know the thoughts of every person in the movie, one would find that people who occupy the same work-family configuration can have very different views on whether that arrangement fits with their ideals and personal goals.

To illustrate the variegated nature of work-family arrangements, consider how the constellations of work and family roles, resources, demands, and personal values are arranged together in the lives of three people. To facilitate understanding of the complexities, accompanying the brief narratives are simple diagrams showing the evaluative judgments (+, -) of the varying magnitudes of work (W) and family (F) commitments. As you examine these arrangements, also consider the extent to which these people compartmentalize or integrate work and family roles in their lives.

Exhibit 2.1   Charlotte—A Work-Centric Professor

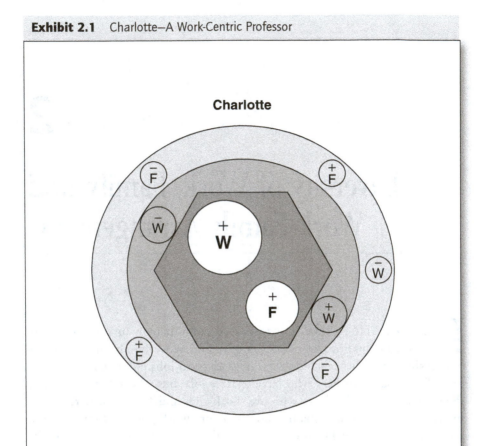

Charlotte is a tenured professor who never wanted to have children. Her mother is deceased, and she is estranged from her father. Her first marriage ended in divorce, and she is now cohabiting with another academic whom she first met at work. She likes nothing more than engaging in her research and pursuing the next big grant. If you went to her office on a vacation day, on the weekend, or in the evenings, you would likely find her there. Her social life tends to revolve around work, and her closest friends are academics. She describes herself (with some level of pride) as a "workaholic."

Exhibit 2.2   Bill—A Manufacturing Worker Who Is neither Work Centric nor
Family Centric

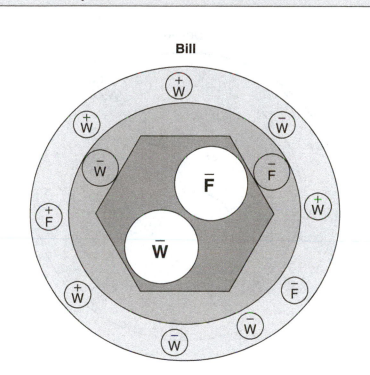

Bill works for a manufacturing company that has undergone a series of layoffs. Most of his old friends have been let go, and he does not socialize with coworkers outside of the plant. He gets little satisfaction from his job, and he drinks too much. Whether his drinking can be attributed to changes in his work situation or not, it is taking a toll on his marriage, which is on the verge of falling apart. His children are in college, and their tuitions are straining the family budget. If he loses his job in the next wave of layoffs (something he thinks might happen), he has no idea how he will make ends meet.

Exhibit 2.3   Devon—A Family-Centric Childcare Employee

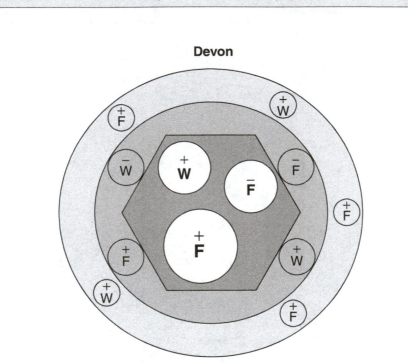

Devon has a husband and a 3-year-old daughter. She is also pregnant. She works about 20 hours a week at a nursery school (where her daughter also is enrolled) and earns $8.00 an hour. Even though her income is modest, the cash she earns is an important supplement to her husband's salary, and she enjoys her job. She is responsible for most of the household work, including cooking, cleaning, and washing. Recently her father-in-law moved into their home (with whom she has had a rocky relationship and who is at an early stage of Alzheimer's disease). His entry into their lives has been a source of stress on her marriage, but her family sees no other viable option.

All of these people have different desires, expectations, and needs. This chapter is about identifying and understanding these variations and why supporting diversity is an essential component of efforts to address tensions between work and family institutions. It is problematic to identify any specific work, family, or work-family arrangement as being "typical" or "normal" or an ideal that should be a tailor-fit social response at the exclusion of others. Instead, responses are better informed if they take into account diversities of contexts that influence how people center their commitments in the workplace or home and the multiple barriers that limit the capacity to achieve personally defined goals. Only then will we be able to understand and address the common and unique concerns of people like Charlotte, Bill, and Devon.

It is tempting to create innumerable charts and graphs to establish the conventional measures of diversity among people in the labor force. Social markers—such as age, marital status, racial or ethnic identity, and sexual orientation—give shape to opportunity and affect both the development of families as well as occupational careers. All of these factors (and others) are predictive of the needs of people and responses to strain (Marks, 2006). And social markers intersect in important ways. For example, disability and divorce have a much greater impact on women's economic circumstances than they do men's. Likewise, age places African American young adults at a more pronounced disadvantage securing high-quality employment in comparison to young adults in general. This shows that combinations of statuses can affect career prospects and family relations. These types of dynamics are well documented and highlight the need to understand the contextual circumstances that may present unique challenges to successfully integrating work and family. The interest here is to draw attention to an additional way of appreciating diversity—that being the variation in personally held values, job demands and resources, and family demands and resources.

Diverse Values and Preferences

The three people identified at the start of this chapter—Charlotte, Bill, and Devon—all want very different things from their jobs and families. Because their values differ, the paths they follow to fulfill their goals vary as well. To some extent every person is unique. However, the "every person is different" argument can be oversold, as it is also possible to identify common career patterns and pathways, such as those that differentiate women's career paths from men's (Pavalko & Smith, 1999; Pavalko & Woodbury, 2000). One commonly offered explanation for these types of gendered career patterns is divergent values and the prospect that women want some things from their jobs and

Work-Family Gender Ideologies

Shannon N. Davis

The belief that men and women belong in separate spheres (public and private, paid and unpaid work) is one of the legacies of the industrial revolution that remains relevant in contemporary American society. From my work in graduate school onward, I have been curious about the influence of a person's work-family gender ideology, or the extent to which someone supports a division of paid work and family responsibilities based on the notion of separate spheres, on the decisions he or she makes regarding his or her work and family lives. Not surprisingly, people who believe that women and men should inhabit separate spheres make decisions about their own work and family responsibilities that are closely tied to their beliefs. However, these beliefs also explain why my research has found a more equal division of housework in some couples, an increased likelihood of marriage among some couples, and a higher risk of divorce among some women.

Where do these beliefs come from, and how are they formed? Individual work-family gender ideologies are internalized cultural beliefs about a gendered division of work and family. They are learned from parents as well as cultural influences. While there are patterns to these beliefs based on gender, race, and social class, they also change over time in response to exposure to new ideas (e.g., education) and experiences (e.g., work transitions and marriage). Given that work-family gender ideologies frame the way that people make decisions about their current and anticipated work and family lives, I believe that encouraging more egalitarian work-family gender ideologies at both the cultural and individual levels can lead to a greater demand for gender equality by women and men in all spheres of life.

Shannon N. Davis is an associate professor of sociology at George Mason University and coauthor of *Methods of Family Research, Third Edition* (Sage, 2012).

families and men have other priorities. But as the case of Charlotte shows, some women align their identities very strongly to their work roles, so it is problematic to make bold proclamations that gender values drive gendered career paths. And when faced with strain, values can guide people to adopt different strategies to reconcile tensions in their lives. Bill's distancing of his identity from his work role may be common among other workers in insecure or low-quality jobs. But one should question whether values *explain* career paths or whether values are *formed by* the contexts in which work and family lives unfold.

Values also influence how interests are prioritized and as such, can play a significant role in the directions that lives take. But beyond this observation, values also influence assessments of the quality of one's situation. For example, if given the opportunity, probably neither Charlotte nor Devon would want to trade places with the other because they want different things out of their work and family lives. And as discussed shortly, sometimes people end up in the same place (such as in part-time jobs, staying at home to care for children, or trailing their spouses to follow their careers) not because their values direct them to do so, but because options to follow their values are constrained. This linkage of values to work and family concerns is complex, and because of its importance, it has been the subject of considerable research and debate.

Gender role beliefs are one of the most common explanations for men's and women's differential commitment to work or family domains. The existing literature amply documents that gender role attitudes affect career goals and strategies, as well as the division of, and attitudes toward, household labor and provision of care (Evans & Diekman, 2009; Greenstein, 1996; Kawamura & Brown, 2010). "Traditional" gender role attitudes assert that young children are better off if their mothers stay at home, that husbands should be primarily responsible for earning the family income, and so on. Those who hold egalitarian values believe that gender should not play a role in determining who is responsible for tasks inside or outside of the home. There has been a strong trend away from traditional attitudes and toward egalitarian attitudes among both women and men. But while values have shifted toward equality, the realization of equality in the division of labor inside and outside the home is not as common as might be predicted from the widespread embracement of egalitarian beliefs. For example, women are still much more likely to subordinate their careers to those of their husbands, and men continue to perform lower shares of household labor (Kulik, 2011; Pixley, 2008a). One reason for these patterns is that structural barriers prevent the achievement of egalitarian goals (Deutsch, 1999; Franco, Sabattini, & Crosby, 2004; Risman, 1998).

In considering why women are more likely to scale back from or exit the labor force than men, values may play an important role. The existence of divergent values held by women and men is the foundational argument of preference theory—that internalized priorities influence personal investments in work and family (Hakim, 2001, 2002). Stirring considerable debate, preference theory is based on estimates suggesting that only a minority of women (estimated at roughly 20%) are "work centered," meaning that their primary sources of identity and value commitments are located in the workplace. A similar proportion, approximately 1 in 5 women, is estimated to be "home centered," meaning that their preferences center around children and family throughout the life course. The remaining 60% of women are categorized as "adaptive," wanting to combine work and family but not totally committed to their careers. In contrast, only 10% of men prefer to be home centered, 30% prefer adaptive lifestyles, and 60% prefer work-centered lifestyles (Hakim, 2001). Because the labor market structures of the 21st-century economy enable women to shape their personal investments according to their values, preference theory suggests that disparities in women's and men's careers are primarily a consequence of men and women wanting different things. This assertion has received support from some studies (e.g., Kan, 2007) but criticism from others.

One problem with preference theory stems from the reliability and validity of the ballpark estimates of women and men who are home centered, work centered, or adaptive. These attitudes are widely variable and depend not only on gender but also on the society studied, the point at the life course in which women and men are interviewed, and the way questions are phrased. The values placed on work and family do not always match up to three discrete preference types. For example, Kathleen Gerson (2001) found that most women in early adulthood typically want it all—career, children, and spouse—as they project their lives forward. Few express a desire to be either home centered or work centered, and those who do are less common than advocates of preference theory assert. But beyond proportionality, Gerson observed that values are shifting in interesting ways. For example, in addition to wanting equality, the children of the gender revolution are recalibrating the importance of having a spouse, child, or career. If faced with the choice of having to give up one of these items, the most common response was—sorry guys—to give up the husband. So while preference theory leads one to assume that values associated with gender are static and fit into conventional boxes, evidence of the malleability and extent of these differences indicates otherwise.

Another important criticism of preference theory has been offered by Pamela Stone in the book *Opting Out?* (2007). Stone's analysis relied on interviews with successful women professionals who had either scaled back or exited the labor force entirely after they had children. She revealed that

The Causes, Contours, and Consequences of the Gender Revolution

Kathleen Gerson

The shift from a social order organized around clear gender differences to one with blurring gender boundaries represents one of the great revolutions of our time. The once predominant vision of separate—and unequal—spheres for women and men has given way to new conflicts and uncertainties about how to combine commitments to work, family, and parenthood. Addressing the sources, meanings, and consequences of this profound social revolution has been the central focus of my work since, as a young graduate student in the 1970s, I realized that, like more and more of my generation, I could not—and did not find it desirable to—follow a life path focused only (or mainly) on marriage and motherhood.

To understand the shifts that have led women into the workplace and changed personal life for everyone, I have spent the last three decades interviewing women and men (in their 20s, 30s, and 40s) about their life paths to and through adulthood. In contrast to prevailing views that the family is in decline and children are harmed by new family forms, I have found that younger generations have largely benefitted from growing up with employed mothers and more involved fathers. In a world where parents are increasingly likely to face uncertainty in their job prospects, marital commitments, and financial fortunes, families with flexible gender arrangements are better equipped to weather the challenges of unpredictable change. While new generations generally support more egalitarian work and family arrangements, they find their aspirations thwarted by time-demanding workplaces and privatized caretaking structures. The answer to today's work-family conflicts is thus not to turn back the clock but to finish the gender revolution by creating flexible job and career paths, community supports for child rearing, and equal opportunities for women and parents of all stripes.

Kathleen Gerson is professor of sociology and collegiate professor of arts and science at New York University and the author, most recently, of *The Unfinished Revolution: Coming of Age in a New Era of Gender, Work, and Family* (Oxford, 2011).

most women who "opt out" of high-powered careers retained feelings of ambivalence—an emotional response not predicted by preference theory. The paths chosen by these women reflected their "preference" but only in respect to a restricted range of less desirable options (such as keeping the long hours in the high powered job but sacrificing nearly all time that could be spent with their children). So in reality the path they chose did not reflect as much what they wanted, as it did a selection made in consideration of the constraints imposed by a limited set of less desired alternatives.

Other studies show that among values relating to work and family, gender gaps are usually small and can disappear entirely after taking into account how specific contexts might promote or discourage particular dispositions. For example, women report lower levels of career centrality than men—meaning that they are less likely to say that their work is an important component of "who I am" or that they would continue working even if financial needs were no longer present. The analytic problem with establishing the causal connection of gender to work attitudes is the fact that women are more likely to occupy bad jobs than men and that workers who are in bad jobs are less committed to their careers than workers employed in good jobs. Once the nature of these types of contexts is taken into account in statistical analysis, the attitudes that women have toward work are revealed to be equivalent to the attitudes of men (Sweet, Matz-Costa, Sarkesian, & Pitt-Catsouphes, 2012). So while some differences between women and men exist, these might be attributed to social contexts rather than simply reflect the outcomes of biology or socialization. Finally, it is important to recognize that variation in values is far more pronounced *within* than *between* genders. Many scholars now conclude that women and men are "converging in their divergences" of what they want from their careers and their families and that the biggest challenge is creating new structures that support the fulfillment of diverse goals (Moen & Spencer, 2006).

When both women and men are so diverse in what they want from their jobs and their families, and when lives are far less scripted than they once were, what should be done to ease numerous work-family tensions? One approach is to act on strategies that limit diversity by supporting and rewarding people who construct their lives to conform to specific arrangements. The conservative Republican politician Rick Santorum (2006) has argued in favor of this position, with a platform that tends to promote gender inequality rather than gender equality. Families that fit whatever work-family configurations are determined to be ideal could be rewarded by policies specifically designed to harmonize their lives on and off the job. One obvious consequence of this approach is that it fails to address the needs of the many families not fitting into whatever ideals the society strives to achieve. To some extent this situation is in place today, as many institutionalized practices and policies are tailored to fit the husband/breadwinner–wife/homemaker model of the 20th century, operating on the assumption that there is a stay-at-home parent to take care of the home front.

An alternate approach is to recognize and support the diverse values toward work and family. To create these conditions, goals do not necessarily have to focus on creating conditions of equality. For example, because traditional gender role beliefs affirm inequality as a positive strategy of managing work and family commitments, those who hold those beliefs can experience satisfaction in their lives as they adopt traditional or neotraditional arrangements (Greenstein, 1996). At the same time, a core element in considering social responses to work-family tensions needs to recognize that most women and men want equality inside and outside of the home. And yet, the structure of work and family arrangements appears to discourage this outcome (Risman, 1998). The fact that women's and men's careers tend to follow different pathways indicates that we not only have to consider the diverse values people hold but also the diverse structures that guide their ability to act on these values.

Diverse Employment

In any discussion of the needs of workers, the most important initial question to ask is "Which workers are we talking about?" As illuminated in this section, the economy is far too diverse to identify a "typical" worker. Instead, what is needed is identification of stress points common to substantial portions of the labor force and the means of easing those pressures by reapportioning the resources and demands that stem from employment. Here are four areas of diversity to consider when looking at the ways employment affects work-family connections: industry/occupation/job variation, compensation, work availability/schedules, and risk/insecurity.

Industry/Occupation/Job Variation

How diverse are the employment opportunities in the U.S. economy? One way of answering this question is to consider the location of people with respect to occupation (the specific jobs involved in production) and industry sector (what is produced). In 2011, the Bureau of Labor Statistics Standard Occupational Classification System (SOC) identified 840 occupations. These jobs range from accountants, to banquet directors, to cardiovascular surgeons, to hand laborers, to package designers, to yeast makers, to zookeepers. The Bureau of Labor Statistics also identified 1,176 detailed types of employers with the North American Industry Classification System (NAICS). This alternate system considers the various types of products or services produced or provided. These range from abrasive product manufacturing, to child day care services, to goat farming, to interurban and rural bus transportation, to newspaper publishing, to vocational rehabilitation services. Just considering these two factors—what people do (occupations) and what they create (industries)—reveals a remarkable variety of potential work situations.

Assessments of the quality of work can differ, depending on whether one is considering the conditions present at any place of employment or in respect to any particular classification of workers. It also is possible for occupation and industry location to intersect in important ways. Consider, for example, how the configuration of occupation and industry influences the compensation received by someone employed to clean buildings (Janitors and Cleaners, Except Maids and Housekeeping Cleaners SOC code 37-2011). According to the Bureau of Labor Statistics, in 2011 there were 2,058,610 people employed in these types of jobs, and they earned on average $24,560 per year. Janitors who work for elementary or secondary schools (NAICS code 611100) earned on average $28,570 per year, considerably more than if they worked for employers contracted to provide cleaning services to buildings and dwellings. Janitors who work for the latter type of employer are classified under a different NAICS code (561700) and only earn $21,960 per year. Now here is where it gets interesting. If a school district wanted to save money, it could conceivably cut its janitorial staff and contract with a vendor to supply workers to clean the buildings. Those janitors, while performing the work of cleaning schools, would be technically working under the classification of providing "services to buildings and dwellings." They would be paid at the significantly lower wage than comparable workers who perform the same duties while being directly employed by school districts, and they would also receive fewer benefits such as health insurance, retirement, or paid time off. This contour of the new economy—subcontracting services—has a remarkable impact on the intrinsic and extrinsic rewards received from work and influences the challenges and strategies of maintaining careers (Osnowitz, 2010; Smith, 2002).

Although occupations define the general range of duties, specific job assignments vary in the degree of emphasis placed on specific types of tasks. For example, consider the work of college professors. This work can involve teaching, research, advising, committee work, and a number of other activities. Professors employed at community colleges earn remarkably less than those employed at research universities, and they are expected to perform much more teaching and far less research. And many colleges and universities rely on poorly paid adjunct instructors, who are hired on a course-by-course basis with no other obligations than to teach. And because each type of arrangement promotes different types of activities, this can have long-term effects on career prospects.

Or consider the opportunity structures for those in the legal profession. Lawyers who work for private law firms can make handsome salaries, but they also are expected to put in long hours, and their career prospects hinge on their capacity to be "rainmakers" (meaning the ability to bring in big contracts). In contrast, lawyers who work for the government or as "in-house" counsel work shorter and more predictable hours. These types of lawyers tend to have greater job security, but they also tend to receive lower wages and status (Williams, 2007). Not incidentally, women lawyers are far more likely to locate into the lower-paid positions, and the transition to parenthood commonly knocks women off partnership tracks.

While it is informative to know the occupation and industry in which labor is performed, it also is important to understand variation in assignments and the ways jobs are structured. These workplace structures vary from worker to worker and employer to employer. Although sometimes workers share common concerns, other concerns are specific to particular subclasses of workers. These observations reveal that the fulfillment of work and family roles may play out differently as a consequence of variation in the ways work is organized and rewarded, even for workers who perform similar types of work or who work for similar types of employers.

Compensation

For most Americans, attachment to the labor force is the means to achieve economic security. But because there is such wide variation in the quality of jobs—especially in respect to compensation received—the economic resources received through employment vary widely. In some respects, we live in a "winner takes all" society, as jobs in the primary labor market not only offer higher compensation but also benefits (such as health insurance, retirement plans, vacation time, family leave). Part-time employment and jobs in the secondary labor market (the "McJobs") provide far fewer resources. But even for those in the winning positions, economic resources are not always as substantial as paychecks might suggest. In considering compensation, it is important to recognize not only the money inflows but also the extent that earnings match family needs.

Wage structures in the United States are regulated in a manner that limits economic security. In 2012, the federal minimum wage was $7.25 per hour, a rate that most analysts gauge as insufficient to achieve a reasonable standard of living. Because of limited access to jobs that provide sufficient work hours or wages, in 2008, 1 in 20 workers (6%) could be classified as working poor. These workers are disproportionately women, racial minorities, younger adults, and the less educated (U.S. Bureau of Labor Statistics, 2010). Calculations reveal that full-time workers in most locales need a minimum of $11 per hour to attain housing, nutritious food, and other necessities for their families. And "living wage" calculations, which are based on the resources needed for day-to-day survival, do not take into account concerns such as saving for children's education or retirement. Because the floor is placed so low, in terms of base compensation, economic need undermines both the capacity to provide or purchase care and leaves many children and aging parents in substandard arrangements (Crouter & Booth, 2004; Heymann, 2000).

For workers in the very wide middle, the quality of life that earnings provide can vary substantially. But it also is evident that even for those with solid middle-class incomes, economic strain is commonplace. Consider, for example, that most middle-class families rely on the incomes of two earners to achieve a standard of living comparable to the earnings that a single earner could have achieved a few decades ago. To accommodate the needs of dual-earner arrangements, families buy two cars for transportation, purchase child care services, and rely more heavily on costly prepared foods. And today families try to provide additional resources to children so as to bolster their odds of success in accordance with new opportunity structures (Sweet & Joggerst, 2008). For example, most parents expect their children to go to college, and parental incomes are the primary source of financial support for students. In 2011–2012 the average annual room and board costs at a four-year public college for in-state students was $17,131, and for students at four-year private colleges the annual cost was $38,589 (College Board, 2011). So while some middle-class families appear affluent, their quality of life may not be enhanced to the extent that a simple analysis of paychecks might suggest (Warren & Tyagi, 2003).

Work Availability and Schedules

In late 2012, the global recession that began in 2008 continues to take its toll. The official national unemployment rate in the United States is 9%, meaning that 1 in 10 people who previously held jobs are currently out of work and actively seeking employment. Estimates place the true unemployment rate to be in the range of 15%, a figure that takes into account people who have given up on finding work, who are underemployed and working in short-term "make do" jobs, and those who are trying to enter the labor force for the first time or to reenter after a prolonged absence (Sweet & Meiksins, 2013). Ironically, while substantial portions of the labor force wish for more work, approximately 1 in 5 workers would be willing to trade away some of their pay in exchange for shorter hours (Galinsky & Bond, 1998; Golden, 2005). Today, conditions of work poverty (not enough work), work affluence (sufficient work), and work overloads (too much work) coexist, and each context gives shape to the challenges and successes of managing work and family roles.

Beyond the availability of work, the scheduling of work has profound impacts on family lives. Today fewer than 40% of employees in the United

Spousal Income Inequality

Sarah Winslow

The past several decades have witnessed the narrowing and reversing of a number of gender gaps. Women are now the majority of college and graduate school enrollees and degree recipients, and, after decades of much wider discrepancies, both women's labor force participation rate and earnings stand at approximately 80 percent of men's. As a work-family scholar, I am particularly interested in what these larger-scale shifts in labor market preparation and experiences have meant for family life. And while there is an extensive body of research examining the causes and consequences of the gender wage gap between employed men and women more generally, when I first began exploring this topic, considerably less work had been done on earnings differentials within couples. My interest was further piqued by heightened public attention at the turn of the 21st century to the growing percentage of women who earned more than their husbands.

Informed by a life course perspective, which focuses on how one's experiences develop and change over time and how the various components of our lives are linked to one another, I wondered about the extent to which wives' income advantages persist over time within couples and what spousal income inequalities mean for marital quality. I found that although a significant minority of women earn more than their husbands in a given year, only a very small percentage maintain that advantage over a period of years. In addition, although much research and thinking assumed that wives' persistent income advantages would be disruptive to family life, my results indicate that marital conflict is highest among those couples in which the income advantage fluctuates between spouses over a period of years. Taken together, my work highlights the importance of dynamic analyses of career and family trajectories and their interrelations.

Sarah Winslow is an associate professor of sociology at Clemson University and author of "The Persistence of Wives' Income Advantage" in *Journal of Marriage and Family* 68: 824–42 (2006).

States work a full-time daytime schedule that approximates a standard 9-to-5 job (Presser, 2003a). Most of this variation is explained by part-time schedules, use of later or earlier shifts, and schedules that vary throughout the week or year. For example, according to the American Time Use Survey, 1 in 7 (15%) of all workers are at their jobs at 7 p.m., and in the accommodation and food services sector the proportion is 1 in 4 workers (24%). On the one hand, employment in jobs with nonstandard schedules can help people serve their family needs (such as constructing a schedule that enables them to receive children after school in exchange for working a night shift; Garey, 1999). On the other hand, these alternate arrangements can introduce strains. As an indication of the impact of these strains, newly married workers who have young children and work nonstandard shifts are *five times* more likely to divorce than comparable workers who labor standard shifts (Presser, 2000).

With these observations in mind, resolution of work-family strains requires considering variation in employment access, the volume of work as weighed against off-the-job demands, and how work schedules overlap with family schedules. Again, in the 24/7 economy one size is not going to fit all workers, and in creating solutions, attention also must be directed to the staffing needs of employers. Accomplishing these objectives will require rethinking fundamental questions, such as how schedules are to be assigned and managed, the length of work weeks, and even the types of community supports needed to help workers manage care responsibilities in the hours in which they are not present in the home.

Risk and Insecurity

Many workers, like Bill the manufacturing employee introduced at the beginning of the chapter, worry about the prospect of job loss. Pervasive job insecurity is not simply the result of the most recent recession or because of global economic instability in general. It is built into the ways that jobs are designed and managed (Sweet & Meiksins, 2013). Whereas in the 20th-century economy it was commonplace for employers to expect enduring relationships with their workers, and to reward job tenure with increased security, these types of arrangements are far less common today. Instead, employers strive to "right size" their workforces to accommodate fluctuating demands for goods and services. Toward that end, there is increasing reliance on contingent workers and shorter-term contracts, as well as for both employers and employees to abandon a sense of enduring commitment to one another (Cappelli, 2008; Sennett, 1998). The variation in the extent of security, as well as the needs of workers as they transition into and out of jobs, is an important context to consider in the work-family equation.

Some workers, such as tenured college professors like Charlotte, occupy highly secure positions in which they have full confidence that their job will be there for as long as they want it. In contrast, most workers are like Bill and Devon, report lower to moderate levels of security. Note also that measures of individual security can underplay the true extent of insecurity. For example, for dual-earner couples, because spouses' work situations are linked, the loss of either partner's job can dislodge both careers (Sweet, Moen, & Meiksins, 2007). And even when individual workers have secure jobs, it does not necessarily mean that their careers will be uninterrupted by concerns such as an unexpected illness or other unexpected events (Hacker, 2006). These types of concerns highlight the fact that risk shapes work and family lives, both in respect to the anxiety it can create and the challenges that result when a winning hand is not drawn (Kalleberg, 2009).

When workers lose jobs, their access to resources varies widely. Consider that most displaced workers have engaged in only modest to moderate amounts of planning for job loss, few have substantial savings to buffer gaps in employment, few have received significant advance notification or pay severance from their employers, and most underestimate the challenges of finding new employment. In turn, these resource deficits exacerbate the challenges of recovering from job loss—both economically and emotionally. However, other workers come more prepared for job loss, and sometimes employers provide advance notification and substantial severance packages. These displaced workers sometimes even report that their lives *improved* following job loss (Sweet & Moen, 2011). These observations highlight that the capacity to form a successful family life is enhanced by the capacity to exert control in maintaining predictable employment. The fact that the structure of the economy introduces new sources of unpredictability requires rethinking the types of supports that people might need to be able to gauge their career prospects, manage gaps in employment, and navigate toward new opportunity horizons.

So while it is true that job insecurity is pervasive in the lives of many workers, not all workers are in precarious positions. And not all employers and workers approach risk management in the same way. These observations indicate the need to recognize the sources of instability in people's careers, the effects that turbulence has on their families, and the ways that they respond to career disruptions. In all likelihood, turbulence is going to continue to expand, along with a further diversification of job opportunities and schedule arrangements. One of the most fundamental challenges in constructing policies is that there are so many types of work arrangements. So long as the normative work situation is misunderstood as a secure 9-to-5 job that pays a middle-class wage, much will be missed in understanding and responding to the needs of workers and their families.

Diverse Families

The beginning of this chapter introduced you to a divorcee but now cohabiting professor (Charlotte), an unhappily married older manufacturing worker (Bill), and a day care worker sandwiched in her responsibilities to provide care for children and an aging father-in-law (Devon). All of these portraits challenge the archetype of the typical family—that of the young, healthy, satisfied, opposite-sex couple made complete with a couple of young children. As Stephanie Coontz (2000) revealed, this image never really conformed to realities, even in the mid-20th century, as far more families did not fit this mold than did. But today the portrait is even further removed from reality. This section provides a brief description of different ways of understanding family structures and how these structures give shape to the work interface. It then introduces the life course perspective, a means of understanding "family careers" and the ways the structural positioning of people inevitably changes over time in diverse ways. Again, it becomes apparent that there are so many types of families and caregiving situations that it is difficult to locate any single or limited set of arrangements from which to pattern or map responses. Instead, what is needed is attention to the sources of strain and how those tensions can be potentially eased.

Kinship Structures

Did you know that if you do not share a residence with your parents, the U.S. Census does not consider them to be part of your family? The reason for this counterintuitive practice is that the Census Bureau specifies coresidency as a requisite characteristic for one to be a member of a family and also requires that family members be linked by either birth, marriage, or adoption. In practice, family is not determined by official standards but by personal understandings of relationships. For this reason, it is common to count others as "family" even if they do not share living quarters and even when ties are not bound by blood, rule of law, or custom.

Understandings of kinship structures as they map onto work-family connections have been blinded by an overreliance on what Dorothy Smith (1993) called the "Standard North American Family" or "SNAF" vision of what a family is or should be. The SNAF archetype of the husband/breadwinner–wife/homemaker affirms broad cultural ideals of the nuclear family and restricts the vision of family kinship ties to the relationship between parents and dependent children and not broader intergenerational or relational ties. Additionally, SNAF valorizes nuclear family self-sufficiency and frames alternate family structures as inferior to this cultural ideal. This type of thinking helps shape, for example, critical evaluations of specific types of family structures, such as the negative evaluation of declining marriage rates and increasing out-of-wedlock birthrates in the African American community.

In contrast, other research directly challenges the thesis that kinship structures are a primary cause of economic hardship and loose attachment to work. Among the most important early studies is the book *All Our Kin* by Carol Stack (1997 [1974]). Stack observed that on the surface, the family lives of poor families in midwestern African American communities appeared disorganized. Children moved from house to house, relationships started and then dissolved, and economic opportunities were forsaken. However, Stack revealed that these behaviors were actually *adaptations* to economic strain. For example, the movement of children between households makes sense when parents become ill and have few resources to manage the strains present. Choosing not to move for a new job opportunity makes sense if relocation would sever ties with kin who provide care for one's children. Not marrying a man makes sense if a marriage to an unemployable person increases family economic hardship (Wilson, 1987). More recently, Naomi Gerstel (2011) examined the ways that hospital workers define and understand family. While doctors are strongly oriented toward the nuclear family ideal, low-paid nursing assistants (disproportionately minority women) rely on wide networks of kin, including parents, siblings, and neighbors, to watch their children. This reliance on extended kin relations, Gerstel argues, is underrecognized in both academic research and public discussions of the ways extended families provide instrumental support beyond the SNAF ideal. Her research also shows that departures from the family structures idealized in the culture are not a threat to work attachment; they are a product of the design of jobs and the ways work is compensated.

Family and kinship networks are critical to the performance of work, but who counts as kin, and the roles that specific kin play in the lives of workers, can vary widely. And because of the reciprocity inherent in the codes of family life, kinship ties are not only resources, they can also operate as constraints. Full understanding of work and family connections, and societal responses to gaps in these connections, requires consideration of the ways people define their families and the options and demands that stem from those relationships. When provision of resources is based on family linkages and family ties to work, this greatly complicates distribution processes. For example, in the United States health insurance is most commonly received as a work benefit, and insurance is usually intended to cover the individual worker as well as her or his family. But what happens when the worker's familial commitments extend to broader kin networks? In most of these instances, coverage is not provided because it is directed to families that conform to a heterosexual nuclear family structure, ignoring kin networks and also in many instances same-sex partnerships.

Caregiving Structures

Caregiving obligations can be brief, sporadic, intense, or prolonged. They can be extended to children, spouses, parents, and broader kin networks.

Work-Life and Parents of Children and Youth With Disabilities

Julie M. Rosenzweig

The challenges faced by parents of children and youth with disabilities when attempting to integrate work and family can overwhelm even the most resourceful. Fluctuations in the child's physical and mental health symptom severity, lack of disability-specific childcare resources, inflexible work arrangements, and stigmatization are among the significant barriers to effectively knitting together these two life domains.

My interest in work-life initially took root nearly two decades ago in the children's mental health field. Parents of children with mental health disorders began sharing their stories about struggling to find work arrangements that supported the exceptional caregiving responsibilities required of them. Many of these parents had been fired from jobs because their children's mental health care and unpredictable crises demanded time away from work. My collaborator, Eileen Brennan, and I quickly learned that these stories were universal to parents of children and youth with all types of disabilities, including physical, cognitive, and chronic health conditions, such as asthma.

Understanding parents' experiences and needs in tandem with those of employers is essential to bridge the gap in workplace supports. While research in this area remains scant, there is growing national and international attention to the topic. For example, a few major corporations are including employees caring for children and youth with disabilities within their diversity initiatives. In support of both research and corporate initiatives, I lead a training intervention and coauthored a training manual for human resource professionals aimed at optimizing organizational responsive policy and practice for employees caring for children and youth with disabilities. I believe that championing this group of employees will contribute to better workplace support for all employed parents.

Julie M. Rosenzweig is a professor of social work at Portland State University and coauthor of *Work, Life, and the Mental Health System of Care: A Guide for Professionals Supporting Families of Children With Emotional or Behavioral Disorders* (Paul H. Brookes, 2008).

And sometimes people are "sandwiched," providing care to younger and older generations at the same time (Neal & Hammer, 2006). As varied as the obligations are, so are the means of providing this care. One means of provision is with hands-on care, performed directly by family members. While care work and housework in general continue to be more commonly performed by women, men increasingly want to be—and are—involved (Kulik, 2011). However, because a significant gender imbalance in care work still persists, a greater strain is placed on women's careers than men's. An alternate structural arrangement is to outsource care work, such as by purchasing childcare or elder care services. In contrast to hands-on family care, outsourced care relies more on the provision of financial resources and for that reason can actually increase attachment to work.

When examining caregiving structures, it is important to also integrate personal and cultural values. For example, it is common for Asian Indian grandmothers to be intensely engaged in the care of their grandchildren, but many American women desire an intense private bonding time with their infants within a nuclear family structure. The issue of eldercare, and the evaluative judgment of the best means of providing this care, is another concern. While some view family as the ideal means of providing care for the elderly, not all do, nor do the elderly always wish to be in the homes of their adult children.

Families in the Life Course

A life course perspective adds the dimension of time to the understanding of family diversity. Rather than solely focusing on the resources and constraints present at any one phase of life, this perspective focuses on the ways lives unfold and how biographies are charted. The key concern of life course research is to understand how the circumstances present and choices made at one stage of life affect subsequent options, choices, and experiences. The questions raised by the study of the life course as applied to work-family recast analysis to focus less on jobs and more on careers (Moen & Sweet, 2004).

Conventionally, careers are understood in respect to work-related outcomes. But the notion of a career can be thought of more broadly to include educational and family progressions as well. For example, many women return to school in midadulthood as a means to reestablish their careers, which are commonly interrupted in order to raise children. Because these women feel that they have sacrificed their careers for the sake of family and their husbands' careers, many feel frustrated in the limited support they receive from their spouses as they embark on new pursuits. So while these women try to readjust their educational and work careers in response to earlier family events, their family systems—with established divisions of labor and routines—oftentimes fail to adjust to the new demands on their time and energy. Key to understanding the sources of their frustration is not only considering their current status (as returning students) but also the paths that led them to this status, their objectives of where they would like their lives to proceed, and how all of these experiences are linked to those of their partners and children (Sweet & Moen, 2007).

Similarly, one can understand divorce as a status, but to fully understand why divorce affects the financial status of women more than men requires understanding earlier decisions (such as those that might favor a husband's career over that of the wife) and also how family structures are redefined in the wake of divorce (such as child custody and child support arrangements). For example, in 2007, divorced mothers were five times more likely to assume custodial responsibilities than fathers, which places greater challenges on mothers in securing work compatible with family demands than it does on fathers. The financial burdens of childcare are not equitably distributed either, as fewer than 1 in 2 divorced mothers (47%) receive the full child support that they were awarded. As a consequence, over 1 in 4 custodial mothers and their children (26%) live below the poverty line (Grall, 2009). These observations reveal how trajectories can be identified by observing the consequences that follow common transitions or turning points, as well as how those turning points differentially affect the lives of men and women.

While life course research focuses on the ways biographies unfold, its concern is inherently sociological, as it considers the impact of relationships at the micro level (such as to children, spouses, and parents) and the ways "linked lives" explain career choices and options (Crosnoe & Elder, 2002). For example, decisions regarding where to reside involve consideration of how all family members might be affected by concerns such as school quality, proximity to jobs, and proximity to relatives (Sweet, Swisher, & Moen, 2005; Swisher, Sweet, & Moen, 2004). The life course perspective also considers meso-level concerns, such as how workplace resources affect options and decisions, and macro-level concerns, such as how social entitlements shape careers over time. The life course perspective also further informs issues of diversity by considering not only age but also how different life stage contexts give shape to family and workplace attachments. Older workers, for example, are not a homogenous group. Some have launched all children from the household, but others have dependent children who are young. Some want to move completely out of the labor force, others want to continue full force in their jobs, and yet others want to have second or third acts and move their careers in new directions. Recognizing the types of diverse arrangements even when people are at similar ages, life course research opens up questions such as "What are the different expectations at each stage of life?" and "What pathways exist to meet those goals?"

Work, Family, and the Gendered Life Course

Phyllis Moen

I began my career investigating differences in the family lives of women who worked part time, full time, or were full-time homemakers. But then I found alterations from one year to the next—part-timers went to full time or else left the workforce; full-timers dropped out or scaled back to part time; homemakers went to work full or part time. Family lives were also dynamic; the women I studied got married or divorced, had babies, saw grown children leave home, and cared for aging parents. This brought me to a life course perspective on work and family—as they play out *in time* and historical context.

Most men aimed to work full time continuously from the time they left school to when they retired. Policies and practices shaping the way work is organized were developed based on men's lockstep life path, assuming workers have someone—a wife—to manage family obligations. Those who could follow this path reaped security, advancement, and benefits. Women, minorities, and the poorly educated were often on the sidelines.

Women's and men's vastly different and unequal pathways represent what I call the "gendered life course." For example, two undergraduates may envision a life together sharing work and family obligations. But because pursuing two careers is hard at best and even harder with children, most couples wind up prioritizing one career, often the husband's. Even egalitarian couples can find themselves on gendered and unequal pathways through life.

Today, few women *or men* can follow the traditional lockstep path in the face of a competitive, volatile global economy and the fact that all adults in a household work for pay. Most young adults don't want a life focused totally on their jobs. Required are public and organizational policies promoting *flexible career options*, so that both women and men can participate in family life.

Phyllis Moen is the McKnight Presidential Chair and Professor of Sociology at the University of Minnesota and coauthor (with Patricia Roehling) of *The Career Mystique: Cracks in the American Dream* (Rowman & Littlefield, 2005).

Summary

Values, employment conditions, kinship structures, caregiving arrangements, and life course progressions are far too varied to create a "one size fits all" solution to the easement of work-family tensions. In fact, many of the existing challenges confronting working families are the result of the enduring institutionalization of husband/breadwinner–wife/homemaker arrangements in an economy where fewer families fit this mold. The need to recognize new types of diversity, and the enduring failure to recognize diversities that have always existed, are primary reasons why people continue to struggle to find ways to harmonize work with family. The challenge that lies ahead involves reshaping work and family institutions—in consideration of diverse expectations and structural arrangements in both domains—so as to enhance the prospect for success.

Useful Concepts

Ambivalence. A state of conflicted feelings as a result of incongruities in what is expected, what is available, and what is experienced (Luscher, 2002). When applied to work-family concerns, ambivalence is a common emotional outcome of the trade-offs made in trying to harmonize home and work lives and the disparities between ideals and experiences.

Careers. The pattern of transitions between statuses. These can be considered both in the family and work domain and can focus on concerns such as timing, sequencing, duration, and turning points (Sweet & Moen, 2006).

Centrality. The degree of importance that any set of relationships has in one's life and identity. The issue of centrality is closely related to observations central to role theory, such as when a person is in a social location but does not invest his or her identity or emotional commitments to the responsibilities expected in that role (Raich & Loretto, 2009).

Contingent workers. "Includes part-timers, temporary workers and independent contractors; those not traditionally seen as entitled to the benefits enjoyed by 'employees,'" or "workers in jobs structured to be of limited duration" (Nowicki, 2002).

Egalitarian gender role beliefs. Acceptance of arrangements in which gender is not used as a factor in deciding how women's and men's commitments and tasks are centered (Davis & Greenstein, 2009).

Kin networks. The set of durable relationships in which people provide and expect access to resources shared among family members (Stack, 1997 [1974]).

Nonstandard work arrangements. Part-time, temporary, on-call, or shift work arrangements that depart from the typical 9-to-5 full-time work week (Presser, 2003b).

Opting out. A reason offered for women leaving higher-paid professional jobs in order to care for children. The phrase "opting out" implies a choice on the part of workers who leave work for family, but many now emphasize that this can be explained not so much as a preference but rather as a response within constrained options (Stone, 2007).

Preference theory. The argument that men's and women's different commitments in the home and work domains are the result of men and women acting in accordance with different priorities and interests (Hakim, 2001).

Primary labor market. Jobs that involve skilled work, higher wages, benefits, greater security, and prospects for advancement through skill acquisition (Piore, 1977).

Secondary labor market. Low-skilled, low-wage jobs that lack benefits and security and offer few prospects for advancement through skill acquisition (Piore, 1977).

Traditional gender role beliefs. Acceptance of the desirability of arrangements that differentially focus women's commitment in the home and men's commitment in the workplace (Davis & Greenstein, 2009).

Issues to Ponder

1. Preference theory argues that women and men have different priorities. If it became a national priority to create gender equality, what would be the best means to eliminate the gender differences in work and family commitments? Note: these initiatives would not only require evening out gender differences in "work centricity" but also the differences that might exist in "family centricity." What specific policies or resources would be needed to accomplish this objective?

2. Suppose you are a human resources director at a medium-sized company. Your company has a family leave policy that "provides for 4 weeks of paid leave to care for the needs of family members," and any employee that wishes to take this leave must apply directly to you. When employees use this leave policy, their absence is felt by the organization, so you have to be deliberate in making sure that this leave option is used only in legitimate circumstances. You also need to be concerned that any decision you make does not set some unwanted precedent (one that might be taken advantage of by other employees) or make employees feel devalued. Identify which of the following employees you would grant this leave to and consider why you make this determination.

   o An employee who wants to take care of her terminally ill mother.
   o An employee (who has a stay-at-home spouse) who wants to spend time with his newborn son.
   o An employee who wants to take time off to care for her husband's terminally ill mother.

o An employee who wants to take time off to care for her niece. This employee says that the niece "is like a daughter to me" and that "her mother is too sick to take care of her."

o An employee who wants to take only two paid weeks off to spend with her terminally ill cat before it is to be euthanized. This employee explains that she has no children and will be as heartbroken when this cat dies as any mother would be. She also cries when telling you this, and you believe that she isn't faking this emotion.

o An employee who says that he wants to spend time taking care of his brother, who has emphysema. This employee has a spotty record of attendance, and his supervisor has expressed concern to you that he might be just trying to get out of work. The employee emphatically denies this.

3. Suppose you have the opportunity to revise this family leave policy that "provides for 4 weeks of paid leave to care for the needs of family members." Based on your attempt to apply this leave policy with fairness, would you make any changes to the way this leave policy is worded or managed? For example, could you define what is meant by "family" or "needs" so as to limit the ambiguity inherent in the leave policy as it currently exists? Or is there a better solution? Would you leave the decision of who gets and who does not get this leave to the supervisor's discretion?

Mini Project

Analyze one of your favorite television shows to consider how the mainstream media present work-family connections. Pay attention to manifest content such as the following:

o Does the family have sufficient economic resources?

o Is there a gendered division of labor?

o Is the house clean, and is there any depiction of the effort involved in keeping it clean?

o At what life stage are the lead characters?

o Is there any frail elderly person present?

o Do any family members have special needs, such as a physical or mental disability?

o Is work presented favorably or negatively?

o Is family presented favorably or negatively?

Then reflect on the latent content of the show, meaning the deep underlying meaning of the characters and its story lines as applied to work and family concerns. To what extent does the show inform or misinform understandings of the connections between work and family?

3

Individual and Family Frontiers: Personal Responses to Strained Schedules

Among the pamphlets at the entrance of my local library is a self-help guide called "Balancing Work and Family." After briefly describing some of the challenges working parents face, this pamphlet offers the following advice:

- Manage your time and set your priorities
- Make a schedule and stick to it
- Plan your menus for the week
- Leave your work at the office
- Get a good night's sleep
- Make time for yourself

Nearly all of the recommendations focus on the difficulties of maintaining a home and a job and how these problems stem from a failure to manage time effectively. The inherent message to readers is this: *The problems that you experience are the result of the way you control your life. If you plan your time, and organize your tasks with care, you can make it work. Others do it and you can too.*

At its core, this type of advice is designed to guide people to fit their lives within existing institutional arrangements. To be sure, people can smooth the work and family interface simply by increasing their personal efficiency and making every minute count. However, a focus on personal response, to the exclusion of cultural and structural constraints, leaves unaddressed the deeper forces that limit the ability to successfully harmonize work and family responsibilities. This chapter shows that personal agency matters, and its application influences the ways work and family intersect. For this reason, it is important to understand how people respond to institutional tensions and the impact that these tensions have on their lives. But also evident are the limits of these responses and the consequences to workers and their families when demands outstrip resources.

To discuss these concerns, this chapter first considers the ways that work and family connections are framed in everyday discourse. Metaphors of balance and juggling guide many responses and expectations, but sometimes in less than fruitful directions. Then considered are the common strategies people use to manage their work and family lives, as well as some of the hidden and not so hidden consequences that result.

Dominant Cultural Metaphors of Connecting Work and Family

In an important little book, *Metaphors We Live By*, philosophers Lakoff and Johnson (1980) argue that everyday use of language gives shape to the way people organize information and channel personal responses. When applied to work-family concerns, consider the implications of the "balancing" metaphor. The solution to the problem of imbalance is to find the right point, centered over the fulcrum, such that one has taken on neither too much weight on the work side nor the family side of the teeter-totter. If one has a problem balancing work and family, this necessitates a sacrifice in dropping obligations from the domain with the heaviest burdens. That is the way the balancing metaphor is conventionally used. However, note how balance also could be theoretically achieved by adding additional burdens where the demands are the least. Solutions to work-family tensions typically do not work that way, and yet the metaphor would suggest that they could. These observations reveal that the balancing metaphor has inherent weaknesses. But the problem goes beyond this.

Consider this situation: a worker reports that he has low "balancing success." His work prevents him from fulfilling his roles off the job, and his family situation prevents him from fulfilling his work duties. The balancing metaphor asks the worker to reapportion his obligations accordingly. But even if he were able to reduce his workload, this will not necessarily improve his quality of life, as giving up some of his work role might require sacrificing aspects of the job he enjoys most (Barnett & Gareis, 2000). While balance is framed as a desired outcome, decreasing the involvement in either work or family domains is not necessarily going to increase personal fulfillment. And note that people who have very few work and family commitments tend to have the lowest life quality. A core observation to be gained from this critique is that the weight of work and family demands should not be confused with the quality of those commitments. It is possible to have heavy demands in both work and family spheres and to have a satisfying life, or to have light demands in both work and family spheres and to have a life of unfulfilled potential. The solution to work-family concerns is not simply a matter of reducing or eliminating commitments as the balancing metaphor would suggest, although sometimes it can be a reasonable path of action (Bacigalupe, 2010).

Like the balancing metaphor, "juggling" suggests that the problem of work-family is maintaining too many commitments, but in this case the work and family obligations are considered to be like balls in the air. Heaven forbid the baby tumbling above should drop to the ground along with the computer and briefcase! Unlike the balancing metaphor, the juggling metaphor tends to focus attention on personal fault, suggesting that once people have chosen to add additional responsibilities to their existing package of commitments, it is their duty to manage the new obligations successfully. When they are able to do so, praise is awarded, such as, "I don't know how she does it!" But when people fail to keep all the balls in the air, the juggling metaphor focuses attention on the choices they made as they added new responsibilities (i.e., to have an additional child or to select a particular career path) or on their skills in handling commitments that others seem to be able to manage. The juggling metaphor does not focus attention to the sidelines, where greedy institutions toss responsibilities to the juggler whether she or he wishes to handle those items or not. Nor does it focus attention to the floor and how that might be designed to soften landings for any items that are not juggled successfully.

While balancing and juggling metaphors are conventionally used to talk about work and family, few people apply them to their lived experiences. If they did, at dinner they would say something like, "What a day I had . . . so many challenges to balancing work and family!" Instead, working parents tend to frame their experiences in respect to the degree of "busyness" and the extent of pressure experienced as they move from task to task (Darrah, 2006). For this reason, many work-family scholars avoid using the terms *balance* or *juggling* except as heuristics that align their research with conventional discourse on overwork and its consequences.

The onus, from both the balance and juggling metaphors, is on the person to make things work and to judiciously select what items to include in his or her balancing and juggling acts and what items to sacrifice. But many of these juggled items are actually beyond the control of people, and among those that are in one's control, choosing to not integrate them can come at considerable cost. For example, consider the parent who wants to see her children succeed. To do so, she might join them in afterschool activities, clubs, music lessons, and sports teams, all of which increase her time and financial burdens. But to drop these commitments may put her children at a disadvantage to children of the many other parents who choose to make these commitments. So, one must wonder, is it in the interests of her family for this worker to eliminate items from the balancing/juggling act in order to ease her personal strains? Or is it in her family's interests to find the tipping point at which she is able to maximize the inclusion of as many responsibilities as possible? In situations like this, one observes a Catch 22, as relinquishing duties can undermine career or family, but assuming duties does likewise.

Work-Family Conflict, Spillover, and Segmentation

If not through balancing and juggling, how is one to understand the work-family interface as it is experienced by people? Scholars point to three distinct, but interrelated, concerns—the extent of conflict, spillover, and segmentation between the workplace and home. These concepts identify the ways that institutional arrangements create tensions, the nature of intersections between domains, and the extent that work and family responsibilities overlap throughout the workday.

Work-family conflict exists when the duties and responsibilities on the job and in the home create mutually incompatible situations. In other words, what a person is expected to do in his or her job directly interferes with family duties, or vice versa. Reasons for conflict can vary. Time-based conflict occurs when work or home duties absorb the hours or minutes available needed to fulfill roles in the other domain. For example, a job that involves frequent travel can conflict with a parental duty to attend parent-teacher meetings or school plays. Or alternately, the schedule of launching children to school can impede the ability to work assigned shifts. Strain-based conflict can result from tension, anxiety, or fatigue from the volume or intensity of role demands. In this circumstance, a stressful job might distract one from being a fully attentive spouse, or a conflict-ridden marriage might distract one from being a fully attentive employee. And sometimes the duty performances expected in one domain contradict the duty performances expected in the other domain—creating behavior-based conflict. Consider how some jobs require workers to adopt dispositions contrary to the attitudes expected in the home, such as the way intimidation is built into the work of bill collectors. The movement from the office to the home for these workers necessitates disengaging from their work selves, as the tasks they perform on the job are contrary to the behaviors expected of a supporting spouse. Each source of conflict—time, strain, and behavior—could suggest different paths of easing tensions in work-family expectations. This might involve changing how much labor is performed, when it is performed, the intensity needed, or the tasks themselves—either in the home or workplace (Greenhaus & Beutell, 1985).

Spillover refers to the consequences of intersecting work and family experiences. This type of interface can result in two outcomes (positive or negative) and two directions (from family to work or from work to family). Positive work-to-family spillover exists when aspects of one's employment enhance family functioning, whereas negative work-to-family spillover is the consequence of a job undermining family functioning. Conversely, positive family-to-work spillover results from aspects of family life that enhance one's role as an employee, and negative family-to-work spillover results from aspects of family life that undermine workplace performance (Stevens, Minnotte, Mannon, & Kiger, 2007). While work-family research tends to focus most heavily on the sources of negative spillover, positive family-to-work spillover is actually more commonly reported than negative family-to-work spillover. In other words, people are more apt to view their family roles as *enhancing* their workplace performance than detracting from it. However, the effects of the workplace on the family are less favorable, as most people view their jobs as simultaneously contributing to, and detracting from, their performance of family roles (Roehling, Moen, & Batt, 2003).

Finally, consider the extent that work and family responsibilities overlap. Imagine two dining room tables. One dining room table remains clean apart from mealtime, and the other has a laptop and a jumble of files that are shoved to the side at mealtime. Or consider two offices, one in which workers can bring their children to work on snow days and the other where family is not welcomed. These types of variations indicate that it is possible to alter the extent of *segmentation*—the physical and mental boundaries that separate work from family (Desrochers, 2003; Nippert-Eng, 1996). For example, if an employer provides on-site recreation facilities, childcare centers, and family cafeterias, employees are encouraged to bring their families into the workplace and to blur the boundaries between work and home. In other cases, rigid divisions between work and family are structured into job designs. Such is the case of the fast-food worker who is not in a position to bring work home. In contrast, freelance writers have discretion over where and when to work and can bring their work home. The next chapter shows the availability of different workplace flexibilities, but note here that what appears to matter most are control and the capacity to customize work and family schedules to fit both personal needs and values.

Not everyone shares the same preferences regarding the degree that work and family are to be integrated or segmented in their lives (Kossek, Lautsch, & Eaton, 2004). This can explain why some (like the author of this book) commute to work even if given the option to work at home. But work and family segmentation also can be the result of structural arrangements that prevent permeability. Such is the case for administrative assistants, who are expected to remain at their desks even if work is slack. And preferences for segmentation or integration are influenced by culture. In the United States, work-life integration is considered a desirable goal for many, but in other societies, such as India, there is a stronger preference to keep the boundary between work and family plainly demarcated (Poster & Prasad, 2005). These observations indicate that the ways work and family overlap can be both a product of structure and preference regarding boundary management styles. Some people develop styles that attempt to integrate and strike a balance between the two domains, others segment—keeping work out of family and family out of work—and still others volley or alternate their commitments between work and family with varying intensity (Kossek & Lautsch, 2012).

Ultimately the goal is to foster synergistic conditions in which the organization of work and family roles strengthens both institutions. A focus on conflict and spillover reveals the extent that work and home responsibilities fail to harmonize, as well as the ways work and home detract from experiences in the alternate domain. A focus on segmentation reveals the extent that work and family roles coexist. In some cases, permeable boundaries might enhance work-family functioning and decrease negative spillover, as might be the case when employees are able to bring work home with them or bring family tasks to the office. But this type of flexibility could also potentially make it more difficult to disengage from work or family roles and introduce other ways for work and family to conflict (Golden, 1998; Golden, 2001a). Finding the path to synergy requires identifying mismatches in the volume of work and family tasks people are expected to perform as well as the nature and organization of those tasks and the personal desires to integrate or segregate the work and family responsibilities.

How People and Families Respond to Work-Family Conflict

When work and family institutions compete against one another, people are forced to make difficult choices, and the culture itself bends to reconcile these tensions. Tensions shift family lives, affect the way interpersonal resources are shared, influence the pace of the life course, catalyze complex acts of coordination, and compel redefinitions of priorities. All of the following practices can be considered adaptive strategies, ways of creatively responding to friction in the work-family interface. While these strategies may ease tensions and expand prospects for success in one domain or the other, they commonly are accompanied with significant costs or risks to life quality, families, or careers.

Doing Without

If work and family commitments are overly burdensome, one means of accommodating strain is to do without—meaning to give up activities or opportunities because of constrained options. Here are just a few illustrations of ways working families are doing without.

Sleep. Today the average American gets only about 6.5 hours of sleep per night, considerably less than the 8 hours recommended by experts (O'Brien, 2001). Some sleep deprivation can be directly traced to work-to-family conflict, attributable to job demands, worries, and the disruption caused by irregular schedules. But family-to-work conflict can create this consequence as well. For example, whereas a stay-at-home parent could catch up on sleep disrupted by a sick child during the subsequent day, in an economy where every adult is expected to work, similar opportunities are more difficult to locate.

Children. In 1960, the average American woman had 3.5 children; in 2011 it was 2.1 (World Bank, 2012). In part the lower birthrate can be attributed to the increased capacity to control the number and timing of children with birth control technologies. However, when American women are asked how many children they would have liked to have, most report wishing they had an additional child (and sometimes more), and the primary reason they did not was because of job demands (Altucher & Williams, 2003).

Care. Children and aging parents often go without adequate supervision because of work demands (Heymann, 2000). The lack of care options, which compels some parents to rely on "latchkey" arrangements, also increases parental concerns of children's safety and behavior. For families on the economic margins, the quality of care is especially problematic, with children commonly left alone and untended (Crouter & Booth, 2004). But even for the middle class, worries are well founded, as unsupervised teens are much more likely to engage in alcohol use, truancy, smoking, substance abuse, sexual activity, and crime (Barnett, Shulkin, Gareis, & Kopko, 2008).

Family Rituals. In the United States 1 in 3 teenagers do not eat meals with their parents at least a few times a week, far less often than children in most other advanced economies (UNICEF, 2007). Family rituals (such as engaging in food preparation and consumption, tuck-ins, walks in the park, and vacations) are mechanisms that bind family members to one another. When work schedules or demands prevent these events, it undermines the opportunity to reconnect and reinforce relationships (Auslander, 2002).

Exercise and Physical Health. Americans live a much more sedentary life today than they did in the past. Although exercise is a vital activity needed to recover from work and family stresses, the more stressful one's work, the less one is able to read the internal signals that motivate healthy lifestyle practices (Sonnentag, 2003). Physical activity is one of the strongest influencers of longevity, but our current ways of organizing work and family commitments discourage this behavior along with healthy lifestyles that include eating nutritious meals (Buettner, 2008). While research on the subject is limited, existing evidence indicates that work-family strain can undermine physical health and well-being (Grzywacz & Butler, 2008; Grzywacz & Tucker, 2008).

Work, Family, and Health

Joseph G. Grzywacz

In a previous life I managed a worksite wellness program serving 1,700 employees and their families. During that time I regularly talked to people, most of who were in blue- or pink-collar jobs, about why they did not participate in company-sponsored wellness initiatives. I frequently heard comments like "I hate my job; why spend any more time here than I have to?" or "I'd like to go to the fitness center after work, but I'm charged $5 for every 15 minutes after 5:30 my childcare provider has my kids." I concluded from these and other comments that constraints of everyday work and family life created very real obstacles to healthy lifestyle behavior.

I have conducted NIH-funded research on the health-related implications of everyday work and family life for 15 years. Two main conclusions are emerging from this research. First, for many, health-related "choices" are formed and executed in a context that undermines healthy habits. The cultural ideal of "working your way to the top," the growing impression that "good parents" expend great energy (and cost) creating experiences that optimize children's development, and structural realities like the expanding 24/7 technology-linked global economy all scream *work and family first, health when time allows!* Prioritizing work and family over health is especially required for women, ethnic minorities, and those in lower socioeconomic positions. The second conclusion is that attempts to promote positive health behavior change require a work-family perspective. Within organizations, "work-life" and "health promotion" need to be integrated to ensure these functions are working toward the same end (i.e., healthy workers). National attempts to affect health, like healthy people, require recognition that policy solutions like pursuing workplace flexibility for all workers is a vital strategy for achieving national health objectives.

Joseph G. Grzywacz is the Kaiser Endowed Professor of Family Resilience in the Department of Human Development and Family Science of Oklahoma State University. He is also director of the Oklahoma State University Center for Family Resilience.

While "doing without" is an adaptive strategy, it can have significant negative effects on personal fulfillment as well as societal interests. For example, epidemic-level obesity rates can be traced to a number of sources, but without doubt time strain is a contributing factor. So long as parents lack the time and energy to prepare good meals, or so long as jobs fail to pay sufficient wages to enable the purchase of healthy foods, efforts to curb this problem will be thwarted. Likewise, so long as parents have limited ability to supervise their children, risk behaviors and their consequences will persist. And so long as people are physically and mentally exhausted, their abilities to successfully contribute to work, family, and community will be affected.

Repace and Resequence

Another way American workers are adjusting to work-family tensions is by changing the timing and sequencing of major life course events. In some ways the loosening of life course scripts can be liberating, as people have increased discretion to decide when to start or stop their education, when (or if) to have children, or when to retire. Changing the temporal patterns of both family and career roles enables an individualization of career paths that can potentially expand opportunity horizons. But the impact also can introduce new challenges, as the life course is now charted in respect to a complex interplay between opportunity structures and personal preferences (MacMillan, 2005). Consider just a few of the ways the life course is being reshaped.

Emerging Adulthood. The lives of "emergent adults" (from approximately ages 18 to 30) are characterized by instable financial circumstances and interpersonal ties (Arnett, 2007). Among these emerging adults are "boomerang children" who leave home but then come back to their parents' homes because of difficulties in finding stable employment. Studies vary in the amount of resources adult children require, but all conclude that substantial proportions of children in their 20s remain reliant on parents for housing and financial support (Arnett, 2004; Gitelson & McDermott, 2006; Goldscheider & Goldscheider, 1999). American culture is still coming to terms with new intergenerational family configurations, as these arrangements present numerous sources of conflict, including the challenge of fashioning agreements on rent, groceries, heating bills, household chores, privacy, visitors, sexual relationships, and so forth (Goldscheider, Thornton, & Yang, 2001).

Delaying Children. In 1970, the average age at which a woman had her first child was 21.4 years, but by 2006, this had increased to age 25 (Matthews & Hamilton, 2009). While access to birth control technologies can explain some of this trend, work opportunity structures also are playing a role. Consider, for example, that many professional women delay having children until they have established greater security in their careers. This increases fertility interventions, as well as increases risks of pregnancy complications. As a consequence, multiple-births rates have tripled over the past 40 years, and cesarean births (1/3 of deliveries) are higher than they have ever been (U.S. Census, 2012).

Prolonging Education and Returns to School. Changed opportunity structures, including job insecurity and enhanced need for educational credentials, have increased the length of time people spend in school as well as the likelihood of returning to school later in the life course. In 2008, greater than 1 in 3 students (37%) could be considered "nontraditional" (age 25 or older; Chronicle of Higher Education, 2010). While a return to school can be personally and professionally fulfilling, it can introduce strains (both financial and time) that diminish marital satisfaction—especially for women who interrupt their careers for the sake of family (Hostetler, Sweet, & Moen, 2007; Sweet & Moen, 2007).

Retirement. Retirement is conventionally understood as the life stage where one progresses out of the workforce and into a life of leisure. Studies show that most U.S. workers wish to retire earlier than age 65 but also develop new attachments to the labor force in the form of "second or third acts" in their professional lives (Moen, 2008). With robust health common into much later years, prolonged labor force attachment may be possible, and financial concerns have made later retirement necessary for many workers. In an economy where most everyone is expected to work, new concerns arise, such as how spouses should coordinate their mutual progressions into retirement (me first, you second? us both together?) and how to sufficiently prepare for financial and lifestyle arrangements that could extend 30 or more years beyond the retirement age (Moen, Sweet, & Swisher, 2004).

The timing and sequencing of the life course is not nearly as lockstep as it was for previous generations, for whom a much earlier termination of education, followed by career formation, marriage, children, and then retirement (in that order) tended to pay off in financial and relational stability (Hogan, 1980; Hogan & Astone, 1986). Today, greater opportunities exist to alter the sequence of key life course transitions. In many ways, this can be liberating as people can customize their careers and create biographies that have unique and sometimes intrinsically enriching qualities. However, old policies and practices designed for the lockstep life course are not well-fitted to the complex and varied life courses constructed today. Career interruptions come with huge penalties, and off-ramps and on-ramps are hard to find for those who want to follow a traditional course, as ways of working tend to be structured for all-in or all-out work commitments. Solving this concern requires thinking of ways to support career flexibilities and the means by which workers can navigate among family, educational, and work commitments not just at one stage of the life course but also across it (Moen & Sweet, 2004).

Fathers and Work-Family

Brad Harrington

Before moving into academia I was a corporate executive with one of the world's leading technology companies for 20 years. My efforts in the work-family field grew out of my personal journey as a global businessperson who faced firsthand the challenges of parenting three young children while traveling to the far corners of the globe. As a father, I often felt tremendous dissonance. On one hand I was the prototypical breadwinner; on the other, I felt I was "phoning it in," far too detached from the four people who mattered most to me.

The Center for Work & Family recently completed its third major study on fathers and fatherhood. What we have learned is both expected *and* surprising, hopeful *and* discouraging, a reconfirmation of the status quo and a glimpse into a new world of possibilities. Fathers are in a time of transition—to seeing their careers and their family lives in new ways. They sit where women did a generation ago—in an established role in one sphere of their lives while struggling for legitimacy in the other. Except this time the challenge is reversed. Men seek their place in the home while living up to career-centric expectations at work. Their search for harmony between these two worlds is frequently challenged by insatiable workplaces, societal skepticism, and their own ambivalence as they seek to find what it means to be a "good man."

Achieving better insights into fathers as they explore their role is tremendously important and can offer rich possibilities for a new landscape in work and family. It may be the most hackneyed phrase imaginable, but clearly "much more research is needed" in this area. Better understanding the experience of half of the world's parents and caregivers is a daunting but noble undertaking.

Brad Harrington is an associate research professor and the executive director of the Boston College Center for Work & Family. He is the lead author of *Career Management and Work-Life Integration: Using Self-Assessment to Navigate Contemporary Careers* (Sage, 2007) and *The New Dad: Caring, Committed, and Conflicted* (www.bc.edu/content/dam/files/centers/cwf/pdf/FH-Study-Web-2.pdf, 2011).

Coordination

The 20th-century husband/breadwinner–wife/homemaker arrangement had a division of labor that made life, if not equally fulfilling, more predictably arranged than in an economy where most everyone is expected to work. Today role fulfillment for dual-earner couples requires a far greater attention to coordination—figuring out who stays home on snow days, how to provide care during school vacations, synchronizing schedules to plan family visits to parents, and determining whose career to follow when opportunity knocks. The following are a few of the ways working families manage these coordination concerns.

Career Hierarchies. The goal of equality in spouses' careers is a commonly stated objective, one advanced by egalitarian values. However, achievement of this objective is obstructed by hard choices, such as those that involve selecting where to live or what to do when family commitments make it too difficult to maintain two full-time jobs. In those circumstances, couples make decisions on whose career interests to favor (and whose to sacrifice) in consideration of factors such as earnings potential, quality of life, and each partner's lifestyle preferences. Once a decision is made to favor one partner's career over that of the other, a dynamic of cumulative advantage is set in motion, such that it becomes more difficult for the trailing spouse to legitimize subsequent equal investments in her or his career. While many couples make initial decisions based on the assumption that they will "take turns" as to whose career will be favored over the course of their relationship, the partner whose turn comes first is at a decided advantage when subsequent decisions are to be made. There are a number of factors that tend to advantage the careers of husbands over wives in this process of establishing career hierarchies, including the fact that husbands tend to be older than wives (and therefore establish an earlier foothold on careers), and husbands tend to pursue careers that offer higher pay. For these and other reasons, couples tend to invest more heavily in the husband's career than in the wife's, even when that was not their initial intent (Pixley, 2008a, 2008b).

Tag Team. Another solution to the problem of parental absences caused by dual-earner arrangements is for spouses to stagger schedules; for example, by having one spouse work evening shifts while the other works morning shifts (Garey, 1999). The tag team strategy increases the missing body problem that occurs when both spouses work overlapping shifts and can decrease childcare expenses. However, it comes with heavy costs in the performance of family rituals that bring all members together. And the nature of spousal contact becomes one of task management rather than shared experience, as spouses spend greater portions of their days engaged in solo parenting (Hattery, 2001).

Commuter Marriages. When prospects of obtaining two jobs in the same community are limited, couples can reconfigure their relationship by living in separate locations. These distance relationships are increasingly common, especially among professional workers. In some ways, commuter marriages offer a benefit of limiting lifestyle compromises that necessarily occur in relationships (such as who gets to shower first). However, they introduce other challenges, such as making parenting considerably more difficult and increasing the expense of maintaining two homes. Commuter marriages are seldom the arrangement of first choice (Holmes, 2009).

Coworking. Other couples resolve career concerns by working for the same employer or by forming a family business. In a historical sense, coworking is not a new strategy, as household economies prior to industrialization and even in early industrialization involved working closely with spouses and children. However, in the current economy, it is difficult for many couples—especially those where both partners have specialized skills—to find meaningful employment in the same locales. For example, nearly 1 in 2 women physicists are in a relationship with another scientist, which introduces a challenge for both partners to locate employment in communities where only one job may be available (McNeil & Sher, 1999). Among academics in general, 1 in 3 are married or in a relationship with another academic. These linked-career concerns make it difficult for a trailing spouse to locate suitable work when a partner finds a job at a college or university, and it presents difficulties for universities to retain or fully satisfy talented workers who also wish to see their partner's career potential fulfilled (Schiebinger, Henderson, & Gilmartin, 2008). Employers are now beginning to consider means of opening opportunities for trailing spouses. Evidence indicates that when these options are made available, coworking couples center their lives more strongly around work, especially if they do not have children or other obligations that might sway them to disengage from their jobs, and their loyalty to their employers may be enhanced as well (Moen & Sweet, 2002; Sweet & Moen, 2004).

The problem for dual-earner couples is commonly described as a three-two concern, three jobs (two in the workplace and one in the home) being performed by two people (Christensen & Gomory, 1999). In fact, the problem goes beyond the loss of the full-time homemaker, as the maintenance of two careers requires additional coordination—figuring out how to maximize satisfaction in the work lives and family lives of both spouses. It is not unusual for acts of coordination to result in imbalanced outcomes, such that one partner feels that she or he has lost out, either in the opportunity to be fully engaged with family or fully engaged with career.

Redefine Expectations

Finally, consider one other approach that people use to resolve time deficits—redefining what they expect in their family and workplace encounters and what it means to live a satisfying life. Here we see some of the greatest sacrifices, as the redefinition of reality commonly levels the aspirations of what our families and workplaces could become.

Change Reference Groups and Role Performance Standards. One would expect that workers with young children would report remarkably lower balancing success than workers who have no care obligations. In fact, differences between these two groups are quite modest (Moen, Waismel-Manor, & Sweet, 2003). The reason why differences are not more pronounced is that after caretaking responsibilities are assumed, workers make adjustments to their other commitments (such as scaling back on work hours or hobbies or other interests), which in turn can ease tensions. Metrics of evaluation also are redefined, such as the standard of what it means to be successful in one's career or family. This can be done by shifting assessments in comparison to new reference groups (e.g., no longer comparing oneself to high fliers) or by shifting the relative value of different aspects of one's life (i.e., recalibrating the importance of idealized work and family role performance). For example, psychological acceptance of a messy household, or a "mommy track" job, can eliminate distress in ways that nonacceptance cannot.

Expect Less From Family. The home has been described as a "haven in a heartless world." But as Arlie Hochschild argues in *The Time Bind* (1997), it also is a source of grinding labor, strain, and disappointment—such as for the tired worker who comes home to a messy kitchen, fighting children, and an equally tired spouse. In contrast, for professional workers the workplace offers numerous sources of personal reward—esteem from coworkers, interesting labor, and engaging conversation. With these observations in mind, Hochschild presents a controversial argument that workers are resolving the balance problem by expecting less from family allegiances and replacing that void with workplace relationships. Rather than seeking to limit work hours in the face of work-family tension, Hochchild suggests that they sometimes use work as an escape from family. It is important to recognize, however, that this analysis is probably only valid for a limited subset of the workforce who labor in favorable work conditions in jobs that offer rewards for creative involvement (Meiksins, 1998). Nonetheless, Hochschild draws attention to the prospect that work-family tensions do not always result in wanting less involvement in the workplace. Sometimes they result in a desire for lower involvement in family concerns, which in turn creates costs to children, aging parents, spouses, or others in need of care and support.

Expect Less From Jobs and Careers. Although the career mystique promises rewards that come from personal dedication to jobs, not everyone is able to secure satisfying work. Sometimes careers are sacrificed to follow one's partner's career, sometimes careers are given up for the sake of fulfilling caregiving needs, and sometimes good work simply is not available. In those types of circumstances, work can be redefined as "just a job," and job holders level their expectations of what they will receive from the work component of their lives (Becker & Moen, 1999). Consider, for example, that some workers actually report *improvements* in their personal lives following job loss. In part, this can be explained by the acceptance of the heavy burden jobs place on their lives. But because the career costs of resigning from many jobs is so high, even from jobs in toxic work environments, workers hang on to these positions believing that they are better off with them than without. It is only after they are displaced that they recognize how much their work was harming their lives (Sweet & Moen, 2011). Increasing numbers of workers are starting to question how central work should be to their lives, and leveled expectations for fulfillment at work may be an emerging trend and part of a generational shift in values.

Redefine Work as Leisure. Fundamental understandings of what it means to work and to relax are shifting in important ways. For example, when folding laundry in front of the television is considered "relaxing," or when cooking or yard work becomes one's hobby, work has colonized new domains, displacing other activities that are more true to the spirit of leisure. And companies are recognizing the opportunities this presents. For example, Wegmans supermarkets (a very popular grocery store chain in the northeastern United States) provide fresh sushi if one is feeling peckish, gourmet coffee if one is feeling sluggish, a model train that loops above the candy shop if one wants to entertain children, and in-store childcare (for free!). On the one hand, the Wegmans experience is positive, as it reconfigures shopping as a family-friendly activity. On the other hand, one wonders about the consequences of other "chores" being redefined as a means to relax and the extent that family leisure and bonding is placed within a broader context of consumerism.

Replace Quantity With Intensity. The ways that work arrangements limit family contact time are viewed negatively by both children and their parents. Only 60% of children believe they spend enough time with their working parents, and 53% of parents feel they spend too little time with their children (Galinsky, 1999). One way to adjust for scarcities of time is to make the remaining available time more intimate and intense. For example, the family trip to Disney World, a week of (very expensive) fun and contact, might be used to make up for absences felt throughout the rest of the year. While escalating intensity can sometimes be used to make up for lost time, it has limits, as children commonly wish for more opportunities to simply "hang out," especially with their fathers (Galinsky, 1999).

Replace Physical Presence With Symbolic Presence. If one cannot spend enough time with family, one can still offer symbolic exchanges that remind family members how much they are loved (Pugh, 2009). This process is exemplified in the Hallmark slogan "When you care enough to send the very best." Providing the latest gadget, the best tutor, or the most enriching summer camp experience can all be means of satisfying care expectations. While the commodification of care can, to some extent, ease the tension in demonstrating family commitments among those who have sufficient financial resources, many worry that this debases aspects of family life (such as the hands-on baking of a birthday cake) as affection is yet one more thing that can simply be bought.

While acts of redefinition can change expectations, desires, and perceptions, one is reminded of Aesop's fox, who walks from the unreachable grapes grumbling that they were probably sour anyway. Reworking what one believes should be attainable from either the home or the workplace is a means of resolving tensions, but it leaves intact the structural conditions that force perceptions to be redefined away from what is ideal to that which "satisfices" in the context of strain. While much of this chapter considers what families are doing in the face of strain and the consequences that it has on their lives, there is an alternate approach, which is to consider what one hopes the family and workplace will become and to identify the barriers that stand between these ideals and the current realities.

Throughout my years of interviewing working families and teaching students about work-family concerns, I have found it exceedingly rare to find people focusing on the horizon of *what can be.* For most working families, efforts are focused on the day-to-day tasks of fitting lives into the existing structures instead of challenging those structures and believing that such challenges have the prospect to create meaningful change. That is the problem with personal agency as it is currently applied to the work-family interface. The major act of redefinition needed is that the status quo is both unacceptable *and changeable.*

Consumption and the Cultural Border Between Work and Family

Allison Pugh

Consumption, particularly the buying we do for children, is an important engine powering the work-family treadmill. Even those who have a hard time making ends meet will go to great lengths to keep buying for their children, cutting back on the basics to do so. I conducted a 3-year ethnography to find out how children came to desire consumer goods and why parents up and down the class ladder prioritized these desires.

Yet even as I knew consumption was important, at first I was loathe to study it, to enter the conversation about our national pastime. Many writers adopt a highly judgmental stance about consumption—as if other people are dupes to advertising, greedy materialists, or indulgent saps who cannot say no. But while judgment has its place in social science—excessive consumption for children is a problem, I think—lecturing can crowd out our capacity to listen and to discover. I found that children used consumer goods to belong at school, to achieve a certain social visibility. Children and parents alike were afraid of difference, even as I witnessed children finessing moments of momentary deprivation with skill and humor. Consumption served as a language of connection, tying peer and parent-child relationships to the fleeting call of fads. Thus while I advocate advertising restrictions, for real change we need to mitigate fears of difference, including teaching tolerance and other school climate campaigns as well as stressing similar efforts at home.

In my current work, I'm again looking at how the economic sphere affects our family cultures. I'm investigating how people talk about what they owe each other—at home and at work—and how pervasive job insecurity shapes what commitment means. Our languages of connection depend on the market, because the cultural border between work and family is a porous one.

Allison Pugh is an assistant professor of sociology at the University of Virginia and author of *Longing and Belonging: Parents, Children, and Consumer Culture* (University of California Press, 2009).

Summary

The "career mystique" promises that an unwavering commitment to work will create feelings of fulfillment. The experience of actually trying to make it all work reveals numerous mismatches between what is promised and what is attained or attainable. The disjuncture between expectation and experience cannot be fully resolved by acts of balance or juggling (Moen & Roehling, 2005). Identifying the sources of work-family conflict, and the ways work and family spill into each other, is a necessary step in identifying paths that move action beyond personal adaptation. And yet, as important is understanding how people and families adapt to work-family tensions. Their strategies—of doing without, coordinating careers, shifting the life course, and redefining realities—show how expectations, behaviors, and cultures are shifting as a consequence of the ways work and family lives intersect.

Useful Concepts

Career priortizing. "The extent to which one or both spouses give greater priority to one spouse's career outcomes in decision-making. It should be distinguished from career hierarchy, which can result from career prioritizing" (Pixley, 2008a).

Career mystique. The belief that devotion to one's work will result in personal fulfillment and the sense of dissatisfaction or disillusionment that accompanies this belief (Moen & Roehling, 2005).

Commuter marriages. "A couple that chooses to live apart and maintain homes in separate geographic locations, with periodic visitation, for the purpose of equal career advancement for both members" (Rhodes, 2002, p. 398).

Coworking. Relationships in which spouses work for the same employer (Sweet & Moen, 2004).

Integration. The extent that people weave work and family together in time and space (Desrochers, 2003).

Segmentation. The extent that people separate work and family from one another in time and space (Desrochers, 2003).

Spillover. The process by which attitudes and behavior carry over from one role to another (Westman, 2005).

Trailing spouse. The spouse who adjusts his or her career to follow the career path charted by a partner (the lead spouse; Pixley, 2008b).

Work-family conflict. "When simultaneous pressures from the work and family domains are mutually incompatible in some respect, such that meeting the demands of one role makes it difficult to meet the demands of the other role" (Greenhaus & Singh, 2003).

Issues to Ponder

1. What is your ideal work-family boundary preference—to be able to access your work whenever and wherever you wish, to have an arrangement that keeps work out of your home and your family out of the office, or to vary between intense involvement in one sphere and intense involvement in the other sphere? What advantages will this offer you? Will there be any downside?

2. What were the most important rituals in your family of origin (the family you had when you were a child)? Who organized and maintained those rituals? Remember that rituals can occur on a daily basis (such as an evening tuck-in) or an occasional basis (such as the family vacation). What rituals do you want to be central in the family you create as an adult? Will or does your work affect your ability to do this?

3. Would you ever entertain the prospect of entering a long-term commuter couple relationship? If you and your commuter partner wanted to have children, what would you then do? If you fell in love with someone who lived far from you, would you be willing to give up your career to move to his or her location (where you might never find an ideal job match)? Would you expect your partner to give up her or his career for you?

4. What is your ideal age to have children, and what is the ideal number of children you wish to have? How are the parental standards you have for yourself different from the standards of your parents' generation and your grandparents' generation?

Mini Project

Make two time lines that extend from now until the end of your life. The first time line is of your intended work career.

My Work Career

20   30   35   40   45   50   55   60   65   70   75   80   85

Enter markers of key life events specific to the work career you hope to chart. Here are a few items to consider marking in.

- Age I complete school
- Age I start my first career job
- Age I find my ideal career job
- Age I reach my career peak
- Age I intend to retire

Now make a second time line of your intended family career.

My Family Career

20   30   35   40   45   50   55   60   65   70   75   80   85

Enter markers of key life events specific to the family career you hope to chart. Here are a few items to consider marking in.

- Age I completely exit my parents' household
- Age I locate my life partner
- Age I get married
- Age(s) I have my first (second, third . . .) child
- Age my parents start needing me to provide care for them

After creating these time lines, consider points of tension where the demands of your work career might outstrip the resources provided by your family, or if the demands of your family career might outstrip the resources provided by your job. For example, if you have already established your work career trajectory, and then find your life partner, can you be assured that your life partner will have a career path that can be harmonized with your own? Might you have to move for her or his career? Would you be willing to move? Or alternately, if your career peaks at the same time your parents are approaching an age where they might need care, how will that affect your capacity to offer the types of care you might wish to provide? And if your career is peaking at the same time your children are young, how will that affect your parental role performance?

If you are in a serious relationship, you might consider having your partner or intended life partner perform this exercise and compare your life charts. Beware, though, you might discover disagreement on expectations for how your future linked lives will be coordinated!

4

Employer Frontiers: Organizational Intransigence and Promising Practices

The SAS Corporation makes business analytic software, products that enable employers and researchers to analyze data and reach sound decisions. Its workforce is highly skilled and motivated. In return for their labor, employees receive handsome salaries and benefits. As the company website (www.sas.com/company/csr_reports/current/employees.html) explains,

> SAS employees are the lifeline of our success. By investing in our employees, we are investing in the long-term future of the company. The SAS culture and approach is based on trust, flexibility and values. Through a healthy work environment, opportunities for development and robust benefits, SAS provides employees with work-life balance. We have been recognized for encouraging creativity and innovation, while balancing work and life. We believe happy, healthy employees are productive employees, and we work hard to create an environment that fosters the integration of our company values with employee needs. As a result of this commitment, SAS ranked No. 1 on the Fortune Best Companies to Work For list in America.

SAS workers have access to subsidized on-site childcare, as well as on-site fitness facilities and health care services. They can drop their cars off for detailing, have their clothes dry cleaned, receive massage therapy or haircuts, and even get their tennis racquets stringed on site. And if they do not want to cook, healthy, inexpensive, gourmet-quality meals are available. It is no surprise that employee turnover at SAS is low and morale is high.

Wonderful as it is, SAS is an exception among American employers. As discussed in this chapter, only a fraction of employers offer compensation, benefits, flexible work arrangements, or family provisions that come anywhere near the SAS way of working. So one must wonder: why is SAS so family responsive, and why are not more employers following suit? To consider this issue, this chapter focuses on what work-family advocates call "the dual agenda"—using family-responsive policies and practices to benefit both families *and employers*. Included in this analysis are the reasons why employers might attend to work-family tensions, the ways that work can be reorganized, and the logistics of moving family-unfriendly employers to becoming more family friendly. Also revealed are some of the challenges confronting employers who may wish to make their operations more family friendly, considering not only the challenges for operations within the United States but also the complications involved in constructing work-life policies to fit a global workforce.

The Dual Agenda: Establishing Positive Outcomes for Families and Employers

Most of the work-family discourse frames solutions as "something that should be done to help working families." The other side of the work-family agenda is providing guidance to employers and helping them understand the ways that family-responsive practices can help them engage their workforces more effectively than the old styles of managing work. The dual agenda hopes to bridge these two interests by identifying policies and practices that serve the interests of families *and employers*. Convincing employers that family demands are not simply personal problems of their employees, but problems for their organizations, is an essential step in motivating them to rethink workplace practices and job designs to fit the complexities in the lives of their current workforces.

Why might employers want to reconsider their organization's talent management practices? One reason is that family-responsive practices can improve many behaviors essential to business success. For example, it is not unusual for employees to miss work because of school holidays or other family-related events. No doubt it is to any employer's advantage to develop strategies that minimize absenteeism, tardiness, or early leaves associated with work-family conflict (Boyar, Maertz, & Pearson, 2005). Approaches could include subcontracting for on-site or off-site care resources, providing employees with options to work at home, or even simply making schedule changes (such as meeting times or locations) that minimize the impact of employee absences. Another reason why employers should rethink work designs is that work-family conflict increases job dissatisfaction, employee intentions to leave, and actual turnover (Allen, 2001; Kossek & Ozeki, 1999; Richman, Civian, Shannon,

Hill, & Brennan, 2008). And evidence indicates that work and family role harmonization corresponds with enhanced affective commitment to work—meaning that work-to-family conflict leads employees to feel less emotionally involved in their jobs (Kopelman, Prottas, Thompson, & Jahn, 2006). Employees who work in flexible arrangements may also do so with greater intensity and effort, in part to "pay back" their employers for accommodating their personal needs (Kelliher & Anderson, 2010). Findings such as these suggest that employers have much to gain by developing family-supportive practices.

To date, the impact of family-responsive practices on workplace outcomes has been less extensively examined than the impact on families, and not all of the linkages have been sufficiently tied to performance outcomes in different employment contexts (Kelly et al., 2008). For example, although it has been established that harmonized work and family roles correspond with job satisfaction, few studies have demonstrated that enhanced satisfaction results in concrete business-related outcomes—such as decreased error rates, increased delivery speed, and enhanced client satisfaction. One challenge in establishing the dual agenda is convincing employers to take a leap of faith on the basis of benefits that *might* result from changing existing practices. If employers can be convinced there are strong odds in favor of achievable gains, or at a minimum that restructuring work will not hurt their bottom line, they will be more inclined to initiate and support new practices or programs. Embracement of this type of cultural transformation, viewing new ways of working as superior to old ways, is one of the strongest predictors of which organizations are most apt to integrate a greater variety of flexible work arrangements most extensively.

Recent studies and ongoing research are making bold steps in establishing causal connections between more family-friendly ways of working and productivity. For example, a series of studies of the Best Buy corporation examined the impact of its shift to a "Results-Only Work Environment" (ROWE). As part of ROWE, employees and managers held a series of meetings to rethink taken-for-granted workplace practices and question assumptions about what happens (for example) when employees leave work early or come to work later than customary scheduling dictated. Employees were granted options to work differently, including having increased control over their schedules, *so long as they were able to get their work done*. Because ROWE was not implemented at the same time throughout Best Buy, this offered researchers an opportunity to study a natural experiment on the impact on "early adopter" work units versus those that were late adopters of the new approach to work (these comparison groups addressed the problem of establishing causality that limited the interpretation of most previous studies). The results were impressive. Employees who were provided with more schedule control reported significantly less work-family conflict as compared to employees in the work units that received ROWE later. Employees in the ROWE units were nearly half as likely to resign or be fired from their positions as those that were not, and these employees were less likely to report that they intended to leave. And the reduction in employee turnover was experienced across all employee groups exposed to ROWE, not just mothers with young children. The new ways of working were especially effective in reducing turnover among employees with greater tenure (Kelly, Moen, & Tranby, 2011; Moen, Kelly, & Hill, 2011). As promising as the results of the ROWE experiment are, employers will want to consider the extent that these practices (and benefits) can be generalized to their operations. One hopes, as more research is performed with other types of organizations, and on a wider variety of workers, that additional evidence will establish the direct impact that specific types of work reorganization have on attendance, commitment, quality, production pace, error rates, client satisfaction, and other concerns that directly affect the bottom line.

An additional question for employers concerns the balance of economic costs and benefits from implementing any family-responsive practice (Drago & Hyatt, 2003; Kossek & Fried, 2006). Because business decisions are commonly guided by the potential return on investment (ROI), demonstrating a positive financial impact is a key consideration. For example, the establishment of an on-site childcare center requires a substantial initial investment as well as a continued budget allocation. If the childcare center has its intended effect, does this investment justify these expenditures? Some impacts can be predicted in quantitative terms, such as the recruitment and training savings from anticipated decreased turnover rates. Other types of outcomes are more difficult to quantify. For example, consider the bundle of family supports that SAS offers. No doubt the array of benefits and perks enhances the prospects of recruiting and retaining the very best employees. But how does one verify that the quality and quantity of output SAS receives from its employees justifies the expenses involved? The items to include in the calculation of this figure may be impossible to establish, as one cannot make a direct comparison to the output of workers that would have been hired if those supports were not present. But even when precise numbers cannot be generated, the positive impact of responsiveness can extend beyond employee performance, as it also can improve the reputation of the corporate brand (again, something that is difficult to quantify in ROI).

With these observations in mind, why should employers integrate the consideration of family concerns in the ways jobs are designed and workplaces organized? The evidence to date suggests that it enhances the prospects of recruiting and retaining the most talented and dedicated workers. There is some reason to believe that it can translate to improvements in production or service provision, profits, and company image. However, because research on

Organizational Cultures That Embrace Flexibility

Erin L. Kelly

Many workplaces say they allow flexibility, but the key term here is "allow." More organizations in the United States have adopted flexible work arrangements like flextime, telecommuting, and part-time options, but managers and employees understand them as optional accommodations available to high-performing workers. Because managers decide who can use flexible work arrangements, employees don't feel that they really gain control over the time and timing of their work. This limited flexibility helps those workers who get to take advantage of it, but it leaves the broader structures of the traditional workplace unquestioned and sometimes fosters resentment among coworkers.

With my colleague Phyllis Moen, I have been studying innovative approaches to changing the organizational culture so that flexibility is embraced as the new norm. We tracked the Results Only Work Environment (ROWE) initiative at the corporate headquarters of electronics retailer Best Buy Co., Inc. Whole teams or departments move into ROWE and are asked to examine the assumptions, expectations, and everyday practices, like commenting on when someone arrives at the office or complaining about long work hours. Employees and managers work together to create a workplacewhere "each person is free to do whatever they want, whenever they want, as long as the work gets done."

We found that employees in ROWE teams experienced less work-family conflict; it was their increased sense of control that brought those benefits. Employees in ROWE teams were also less likely to leave the company or be planning to leave in the near future. These employees began taking better care of themselves by sleeping more, not coming to work when sick, and going to the doctor even when they're busy. The research points to the benefits of broadening access to newer ways of working and embracing flexibility as a central part of the organizational culture.

Erin Kelly is associate professor of sociology at the University of Minnesota and author (with Phyllis Moen and Eric Tranby) of "Changing Workplaces to Reduce Work-Family Conflict: Schedule Control in a White-Collar Organization" in *American Sociological Review* 76: 265–90 (2011). See gorowe.com for more information on ROWE.

Family Supportive Work Environments

Ellen Ernst Kossek

Growing numbers of employees need to access family-supportive work environments. My research reveals that family-supportive work environments are comprised of three factors: a job design that gives employees control over where and when they work, supportive managers, and a family-support-ive organizational culture. My early studies showed that although managers are sometimes reluctant to value family-supportive policies such as flextime that gives employees higher control over work hours, employees view flextime as the most innovative of all human resource practices. I also  found that employees who use employer-supported on-site childcare are more likely to return to work earlier after maternity leave and are less likely to leave their employer. Employees receiving childcare support also feel more positive about their abilities to perform their jobs well and care for their families.

Recently, with Leslie Hammer, I developed a training program that teaches retail managers how to be more family supportive. We identified four kinds of supportive behaviors: emotional support (showing care about employees' fam-ily lives); structural support (providing flexibility to resolve work schedule conflicts); role modeling (modeling positive attention to family and work); and creativity (working with other managers to cross-train employees to increase storewide flexi-bility overall). Through our efforts to teach managers to be responsive to employees' family needs, we observed that sometimes seemingly small supportive actions can make a tremendous difference in employees' lives. For example, simply inquiring about how an employee's family is doing can catalyze supportive behaviors.

Overall, my research studies have shown that family-supportive work envi-ronments can be created by giving employees access to flextime, helping them find quality childcare, and training managers. Family-supportive workplaces are occupational pathways to worker and family effectiveness and can poten-tially benefit employers in the long run.

Ellen Ernst Kossek is university distinguished professor at Michigan State University. She has written many referred articles on work and family and authored or edited 9 books, including *CEO of Me: Creating a Life That Works in the Flexible Job Age* (Pearson Education, 2008).

work outcomes remains limited, there is some level of faith involved in any decision to reconfigure work designs. When considering the balance of risk, for many employers a greater hazard lies on the side of continued use of rigid work designs constructed in the old husband/breadwinner–wife/homemaker economy. In the economy where most everyone works, home is inevitably going to be a source of persistent disruption at work. Reconfiguring work expectations and flexibilities that facilitate the performance of family roles requires rethinking taken-for-granted standards of what it means to be an ideal employee.

Availability and Use of Employer-Provided Family-Responsive Policies and Practices

One of the most promising ways to facilitate work-life integration is to extend greater flexibility to workers in where, when, how, or how much work is to be performed. For example, rather than requiring workers to clock-in and clock-out at set times and perform all of their work on site, a flex-time arrangement can enable some employees to begin their work earlier or later than is customarily expected, or a flex-place arrangement can enable some employees to perform some or all of their work off site. Assessing the availability and use of these types of arrangements is complicated by the distinction between "formal availability" (meaning that is on the books and ostensibly open for use) and "informal availability" (meaning that interpersonal relations sway access to use). Either measure indicates that access to, and use of, flexible work arrangements is limited and unevenly distributed.

Studies show that flexible work arrangements, whether formal or informal, are usually available only to some classifications of workers and neglect especially the needs of lower-status employees (Golden, 2001b; Swanberg, Pitt-Catsouphes, & Drescher-Burke, 2005). This illustrates the dynamic that sociologists label "the Matthew effect" (named after a passage in the Gospels)—*those who have shall receive* (Merton, 1968). The segments of the workforce with the fewest needs (men and upper-status workers) also have access to the most resources to manage those needs. Because women are more likely to be employed in lower-status positions, they actually have a *lower* likelihood of receiving access to flexible work arrangements than men. However, when access is available, women are more likely to use flexible work arrangements than men, although oftentimes at considerable costs to their careers.

How frequently do employers formally provide flexible work arrangements to their employees? Determining the answer requires considering two factors: type of flexibility and the threshold at which an option is considered available. Most studies consider a flexible work arrangement as being available if it is

Facets of Workplace Flexibility—Implications From the Multiple Dimensions of Working Time

Lonnie Golden

The roots of my personal perspective probably go back as far as being a teen employee in a supermarket with an unsympathetic manager and also working for a year in a communal-type farm enterprise. I eventually embarked on a career as a labor economist, still integrating my own experiences with economic theories. After attempts to analyze causes in the long-term trends in working hours in the labor market, and their effects on employment, I gradually became interested also in the consequences of work hours on people's well-being, families, and workplaces. Time at work is associated not only with income but also identities and roles, both daily and over the life cycle.

I study all dimensions of working time—its duration and its responsiveness to employers' and employees' preferences, i.e., its "variability" and "flexibility," respectively. Staying true to my inner economist, I tend to rely on large-sample data sets and econometric techniques. I find compelling the three-prong stool of theory, empirical testing, and policy formulation. My work attempts to address all three. A case in point is the clear irrationality of both overemployed and underemployed workers in the same occupation, industry, or even workplace. My theoretical side demonstrates how these conditions may persist, which workers are most afflicted by either state, and how innovative public policy reform could help redress this at the national and even organizational level, to make more people better off in a way that is cost neutral to employers and facilitates long-term productivity. The future belongs to such flexibility for workers—such as a right to refuse overtime work, under certain conditions, for which I've advocated and that has been adopted by certain states for certain occupations.

Lonnie Golden is professor of economics and labor studies, Penn State, Abington, and author of "Not Formally Introduced? Formal vs. Informal Flexible Daily Work Schedules among US Workers," *Industrial Relations*, *48*(1), January 2009, 27–54.

open to "any" employees in the organization (i.e. Davis & Kalleberg, 2006). However, the implications of using this lenient standard can lead to a dramatic overestimation of true availability, because an organization that offers arrangements to only 1 percent (or less) of its workforce could be classified as providing flexibility. Additionally, the type of flexibility offered is important, as this can take multiple forms, including discretion to change when or where work is performed or other options such as scaling back on work hours.

To provide estimates of formal availability, Exhibit 4.1 shows the amount of flexibility available using two measures, availability to some employees (the most common standard used) and availability to most or all employees, meaning that the majority of the employer's workforce has access to a particular type of flexible work arrangement. Arrangements fall into three broad categories: move-work arrangements, reduce-work arrangements, and pause-work arrangements. The option to move work means that employees can request a change in their schedule, such as starting and quitting times or compressed workweeks, or work location, such as working from home or at different worksites. All of these approaches share the option of altering where or when work is to be performed. Reduce-work arrangements include programs and practices providing the option to limit work hours, work part time at the same position or level, job share, phase into retirement, or work part year for a

Exhibit 4.1 Percentages of American Employers Who Make Flexible Work Arrangements Available to Some, Most, or All Employees.

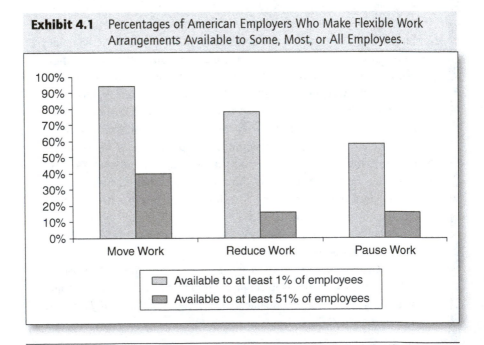

Source: Author's Analysis of the 2009 Talent Management Study (*N*=696 U.S. Employers)

reduced amount of time. All of these approaches share the option of reconfig-uring the volume of work to be performed. Pause-work arrangements include programs and practices providing the option to request career breaks or sab-baticals, or paid or unpaid time for education or job training.

Exhibit 4.1 shows the remarkable variation in flexible work availability within organizations, as well as the limited extent options are available to most or all workers. While it is true that most organizations make one or more flex-ible work arrangements available, most organizations do not make them avail-able to the majority of their workforces. Thus most workers (especially those in lower-level positions) do not have the capacity to adjust work arrangements in ways made available to limited numbers of their coworkers. And when flex-ible work arrangements are made available, they most commonly enable employees to move when or where they do their work (i.e., earlier or later in the day, on the weekends, at home) but not the volume of work they are expected to perform (i.e., reduced work for less pay, a temporary break from work). This way of implementing flexibility leaves most employees at most organizations caught in time binds when family needs are high or escalate.

In practice, most flexible work arrangements are informally negotiated individually between employees and their supervisors (Golden, 2009; Kelly & Kalev, 2006; Wharton, Chivers, & Blair-Loy, 2008). But when a formal policy exists, although it is technically available, it does not necessarily mean it is perceived by employees as being usable (Barnett, Gareis, Gordon, & Brennan, 2009; Eaton, 2003; Lambert, Marler, & Gueutal, 2008). For example, profes-sional workers might have an option to reduce their work hours but know that if they do so, they could be moved off a career track and their work may be restricted to the least rewarding tasks. Therefore, even though they could technically take a reduced-hours schedule, they do not view the option as an effective resource, as the penalties for actual use are prohibitively high. In other circumstances, workplace cultures can trump formal policies. In these contexts, even when workers technically have the right to request an alternate arrangement, this request might be met with other sanctions that leave work-ers afraid for their jobs or careers (Hochschild, 1997).

While many workplaces remain attached to rigid 9-to-5 full-time employment, others are implementing alternate schedule arrangements and testing the advantages that might be offered. These include job-sharing arrangements in which two employees assume the responsibilities of one position and coordinate their efforts with the benefit of each being required to work shorter hours. Other organizations have moved to compressed four-weekday schedules, with employees working longer hours each day in return for an extra day off on the weekends. This has been met favorably by many workers and also saves employers related expenses such as electric and heating costs (Wadsworth, 2009).

Beyond flexibility and altered schedule arrangements, employers also can provide other direct resources to families such as onsite childcare facilities. While these facilities can relieve work and family conflict, they are only available at a small portion of work sites (Connelly, Degraff, & Willis, 2002). Estimates indicate that fewer than 1 in 10 American employers (with 100 or more employees) have on-site childcare centers, and when they are available, they are limited in the number of employees served. This type of resource is far less common among smaller employers (Friedman, 2001). Few small employers can provide on-site childcare, and even if they could, many work environments are not hospitable to children. Employers also can provide indirect resources (such as pretax flexible savings accounts that make childcare more affordable). More commonly employers provide informational resources, such as occasional work/life seminars, or contract for resource and referral sources that help employees locate service providers. While these lower-cost informational resources may potentially help some employees, they have been critiqued as little more than window dressing compared to more resource-intensive approaches needed to resolve work-family conflicts. Consider, for instance, the difference between providing workers with access to a counselor who might help them locate an elder care provider versus providing them with wages or benefits sufficient to pay for the services located.

Some employers are integrating flexible work arrangements and extending resources to employees in ways that can facilitate work-life integration. However, most workers labor in jobs that do not offer the resources needed to substantially reduce work-family conflicts. But beyond overall availability, the uneven ways employers allocate family-responsive resources to segments of their workforces remains a concern, as does the uneven availability across industry sectors. The evidence indicates that expanded flexibility is needed not only in the number and variety of formal options on the books, but also in the cultural acceptance of these options so that they can be used without penalty. And beyond broadening the array of flexible work options, attention needs to be directed to expanding the opportunities to broader segments of the workforce.

Process of Organizational Change: Moving From Awareness to Action

One reason why employers should move toward family-responsive practices is that it may be in their best interests to do so. But what social mechanisms compel employers to strive to be more family friendly? Adaptation theory and institutional theory both offer important insights, as they help one understand how organizations might move to action.

Adaptation theory focuses on economic principles related to environmental pressures that drive employers to innovate (Milliken, Dutton, & Beyer, 2002; Pfeffer & Salancik, 1978). If, for example, an employer relies on scarce labor supplies, this pressure could motivate it to institute new programs to become an "employer of choice" in order to attract the very best talent away from the competition. This process likely is in play for companies such as SAS, as the value of employees can be very high, as are the replacement costs from employee turnover. Any effort to attract and keep the best talent can be considered a strategic response. Adaptation theory also helps explain why other employers offer few benefits, low wages, and virtually no family supports. Most of these employers, those that fit the McDonalds archetype, rely on workers who are easily replaced. In those contexts, external pressures are minimal, and readjusting practices or reward structures will have little return and might actually increase costs. These constraints can explain why access to resources such as flexible work vary significantly across organizations and why one should not expect a business case to move all employers to become family responsive. The business case, for many employers, is to be family unresponsive.

In contrast, *institutional theory* considers organizations as responding to a variety of social pressures from within the organization, such as the demographics of the labor force or the values embraced by key decision makers (DiMaggio & Powell, 1983; Kelly, 2003; Meyer & Rowan, 1977). For example, if an organization has a significant number of women in leadership positions, their presence helps them influence the prioritization and structure of family-friendly policies (Hutchens & Grace-Martin, 2006; Moshavi & Koch, 2005; Wood, de Menezes, & Lasaosa, 2003). While adaptation theory focuses primarily on the economic motivators for change, institutional theory draws additional attention to the expectations that workers and other stakeholders may have and the impact that workplace culture has on taken-for-granted ways of working. One often-cited example of this process is the case of Hewlett Packard, which in the 1980s instituted a variety of options to employees—including job sharing, flexible work schedules, and telecommuting—well ahead of its competitors. These changes came under the direction of CEO Lew Platt, who felt firsthand the conflicts of work and family (that many CEOs are shielded from) in the aftermath of his wife's death. Hewlett-Packard did not change because it necessarily needed to; it changed because a leader within the organization believed it should for both business and employee interests.

Research That Leads to Action at the Families and Work Institute

Ellen Galinsky

When I cofounded the Families and Work Institute in 1989, our mission was to conduct research that "informs" action on the changing workforce, family, and community. To do so, we established two major nationally representative studies—one of employees, the other of employers. Our National Study of the Changing Workforce, launched in 1992 and replicated every 5 to 6 years, is the most comprehensive ongoing investigation of the U.S. workforce's lives on and off the job. Our National Study of Employers, launched in 1998 and conducted every 3 to 4 years, is likewise the most comprehensive ongoing investigation of the practices, policies, and benefits provided by U.S. employers to address the changing needs of today's workforce and workplace.

These parallel studies have been widely used by policy makers, employers, and academics. For example, we created measures to assess "supervisor support for work life" and "organizational work-life culture" and found that employers subsequently adopted practices to address these issues. But taking action was left to others, and that felt unsatisfactory to us.

In 2003, we had the opportunity to do research that leads to action, thus expanding our mission. With funding from the Alfred P. Sloan Foundation, we launched When Work Works, based on a theory of change. When Work Works is now a joint project of the Society for Human Resource Management and the Families and Work Institute. Working with community partners across the country who conduct local educational and media outreach, we highlight and honor effective practices through the Sloan Awards for Excellence in Workplace Effectiveness and Flexibility. Our ongoing evaluations show that this project has helped change the message so that workplace flexibility is not a perk but a business tool and has helped catalyze transformations in employment practices. Importantly for us, it gives the ongoing opportunity to use a research-based approach to improve workplaces.

Ellen Galinsky is the cofounder and president of Families and Work Institute and coauthor of "From Research to Action in Workplace Flexibility: Lessons in Bringing About Workplace Change" in *The Future of Children* Vol. 21, No. 2 (Princeton University and the Brookings Institution, 2011).

Research supports that organizations are responding because they have to (adaptation theory) and because stakeholders want them to (institutional theory). Organizations are far more family responsive than they were just a few decades ago in part because they need to be and in part because workers and their employers believe in the merits of these changes. However, the trajectory for future voluntary change on the part of employers is going to depend on the amount of pressure placed on organizations (both internally and externally), the resources at their disposal, and cultural standards of what constitutes reasonable terms of employment. Studies show that some factors, such as the percentage of unionized or older workers, are not moving employers to be as family responsive as either institutional theory or adaptation theory would predict (Davis & Kalleberg, 2006; Matz-Costa & Pitt-Catsouphes, 2010). Findings such as these, along with the uneven availability of employer-based family-responsive practices, indicate a need to also consider and adjust the general regulatory constraints in which employers operate (the subject of the remaining chapters).

Finally, consider not only the types of work-family policies enacted, but also how they are framed and presented within organizational contexts. For example, how might a nonparent employee react to being denied an option to work at home if that option is granted to a coworker because she is a parent? While employer-based family-friendly policies offer workers the prospect of additional resources, employees can resist (or even react negatively to) implementation if these policies are viewed as unfairly advantaging one group of workers over others (Smithson, 2006). This observation requires considering aspects of organizational justice in both defining policy and presenting it to employees. Formulation of communications strategies should include reflections on the extent that any policy or program treats all employees fairly, information about how the policy demonstrates this fairness, and standards set forth to ensure that employees who take advantage of a program or policy are treated with equal respect and dignity (Trefalt, 2010).

In some circumstances, there may be good reasons to restrict access to specific programs to limited classifications of workers. However, in respect to interpersonal justice in the workplace, so long as a policy offers resources to one group of employees (e.g., on the basis of the ages of their children, sexual orientation of their partner, elder care responsibilities), it may be viewed by other employees (e.g., nonparents) as operating at their expense and as a result potentially undermine the organization's effectiveness rather than enhance it. For that reason, employers will likely maximize advantages when they make decisions about their employees' job expectations not so much on unique or specific family situations, but rather on their capacity to perform work. In that way, the employee who wants to take time out to coach a son's or daughter's sports team will be treated with the same fairness as the coworker who wishes to go sailing or train for a marathon.

Another approach of increasing equity among diverse employees is to move from defined-benefits plans (that provide rigid allocations of resources) to cafeteria-style plans. These cafeteria plans provide workers with a wide set of fringe benefits to select from, and they make choices based on the benefits that best work for their personal needs. For example, one employee might move some proportion of her or his benefit money into life insurance that will provide benefits to her or his family, but another employee might move that money into a personal retirement account. Because employees can tailor allocations to fit their specific personal and family needs, they are positioned to receive different, but comparable, compensation from their employer. In turn, the concern of some employees getting more than others because of their family situation is averted.

In some instances, the structure of organizations can be changed so that employees can set their own priorities and negotiate them against those of their coworkers. For example, a number of hospitals are now using "self-scheduling" systems in which employees designate the shifts they cannot work, those they are not interested in working, and those they particularly prefer. The software has the potential to fit employees into their most desired schedules, as well as identify shifts that need additional staffing. When vacancies appear, employees can bid on those work opportunities and indicate their interest in working an undesired shift for additional pay or in return for other types of compensation. For the hospital, this offers the prospect of easing the work of staffing shifts that might vary from week to week, and employees would not be locked into rigidly defined, overly constricting schedules. Although this type of approach may offer promise, results are inconclusive that it eases work-family tensions, as the self-scheduling systems can introduce week-to-week variation that can be disruptive to employees' lives, and the schedules that employees prefer are not always ultimately assigned (Bailyn, Collins, & Song, 2007). But other studies indicate that increasing worker control to negotiate schedule preferences with fellow employees can affect positive outcomes on concerns such as absenteeism (Lambert, 2009). Flexibility is needed but also predictability—for both the employer and employee.

The process of moving employers to become more family friendly requires changing organizational understandings of work- and family-related values. Support from key leaders is an essential ingredient, but pressures can be exerted by other entities within and beyond the organization. To some extent, organizations can be expected to operate in their self-interest. However, the speed with which they change, and the extent to which they drive toward new horizons, may be dependent on expanding expectations, demonstrating alternate ways of organizing work, and highlighting practices evident among other (prosperous) employers.

Rethinking the Scheduling of Work

Researchers at the Sloan Center on Aging & Work have been exploring options that might facilitate the engagement of workers in the health care sector. Workers in this sector—including nurses, pharmacists, social workers, and housekeeping staff—commonly report working long hours, with schedules that lack predictability or stability. For employers, the consequences of poor schedule fit include higher labor turnover rates and decreased capacities to provide the highest-quality care. For example, because of scheduling challenges, shifts are sometimes only partially staffed, in part because employees are reluctant to work additional hours when needs emerge. As a result, it takes hospitals longer to provide patients with care, and the services patients receive may be less than satisfactory. For workers, poor schedule fit results in lower job satisfaction, diminished appraisals of work-life balance, and difficulties in managing responsibilities off the job. To consider how work might be done differently, the Sloan Center on Aging & Work examined different scheduling practices among hospitals that gained recognition as leading-edge employers. Their findings are shown in Exhibit 4.2.

One important contribution of research on various scheduling practices is the finding that alternate time management strategies can result in benefits for both employees and their employers, fulfilling the dual agenda. Most commonly, alternative scheduling practices improved employee retention and the employer's ability to attract talent. These work arrangements also enhanced team performance, work-life schedule fit, and employee attitudes toward their jobs. However, also note that all of these scheduling approaches introduced new challenges. One concern relates to fairness and the need to create policies that treat employees in an equitable manner. Related to this issue is the prospect that the hospitals sometimes had to deny the specific schedule requests of employees, either because of the employee's unique position or because of particular staffing needs. In many ways these alternative scheduling practices complicated the assignment of workers to specific time slots and introduced new variations in shift construction. However, because preexisting rigid systems complicated the performance of family responsibilities, the new scheduling approaches may have simply transferred where the complexities are shouldered, moving them out of the family domain and into the work domain.

Employers in other sectors of the economy may be able to take bolder or weaker steps than those discussed here as they are practiced in the

Exhibit 4.2   Some Promising Scheduling Practices Identified Among Award-Winning Health Care Sector Employers

Manager-Initiated Discussions of Schedule Fit

Description: Required discussions about flexibility between supervisors and staff; supervisors and staff may work from a menu of options; supervisors request feedback from staff about alternate work options.

Common Benefits: Increased communication between staff and management; improved retention and ability to attract talent; improved work-life balance scores; improved business outcomes.

Common Challenges: Balancing requests for flexibility with need to maintain staffing levels; handling situations in which requested options cannot be granted.

Phased Retirement

Description: Gradual reduction of hours to older workers over a specified time frame, with a possible change in responsibilities.

Common Benefits: Organization prevents or slows brain drain; older workers gain some of the benefits of retirement and also maintain a connection to the organization; improved work-life balance scores; improved business outcomes.

Common Challenges: Balancing requests for different work options by older workers with the need to maintain staffing levels; handling situations in which requested options cannot be granted; constraints emanating from the Employee Retirement Income Security Act (ERISA); achieving equity across age groups.

Employee Input Into Scheduling

Description: Staff can select the days on the upcoming schedule that they want to work.

Common Benefits: Staff are able to select a schedule that fits their work and personal lives; improved retention and ability to attract talent; improved work-life balance scores; improved business outcomes.

Common Challenges: Balancing requests for flexibility with need to maintain staffing levels; handling situations in which requested options cannot be granted; constructing well-defined scheduling procedures.

Job Sharing

Description: Two employees share a single position.

Common Benefits: Improved retention and ability to attract talent; improved work-life balance scores; improved team environment; improved business outcomes.

Common Challenges: Handling situations where one of the two participants does not abide by the agreement or fails to meet expectations; addressing conflict issues between pairs of employees; creating an equitable and mutually agreeable mechanism for matching equally qualified employees.

Flexible Scheduling

Description: Staff can request changes in starting/quitting times on a daily basis or from time to time.

Common Benefits: Staff are able to select a schedule that fits their work and personal lives; improved retention and ability to attract talent; improved work-life balance scores; improved business outcomes.

Common Challenges: Balancing requests for flexibility with need to maintain staffing levels; handling situations in which requested options cannot be granted; constructing a well-defined policy; addressing perceptions of favoritism.

Compressed Work Week Schedules

Description: For example, three 12-hour days or four 10-hour days.

Common Benefits: Staff are able to select a schedule that fits their work and personal lives; improved retention and ability to attract talent; improved work-life balance scores; improved business outcomes.

Common Challenges: Balancing requests for different work options with the need to maintain staffing levels; handling situations in which requested options cannot be granted, either in total or part; constructing a well-defined policy; addressing perceptions of favoritism.

Note: Special thanks to Marcie Pitt-Catsouphes, Kevin Cahill, Suzanne Lawler, and Jacqueline James for the research presented.

health care sector, considering not only when work occurs, but also where it is to be performed. There is reason for optimism, and as employers develop new time and place management strategies, productivity and the lives of their employees' families will likely benefit. But these innovations necessarily require accepting risk and understanding that the current ways of organizing work are not the only ways available.

Flexible Work in Multinational Organizations

Multinational employers set up operations across countries and as a consequence face challenges in managing global workforces. Some of these employers are wrestling with recruiting and retaining a diverse workforce and have linked these efforts to considering ways of making their global operations more family friendly. These companies, however, are finding many unexpected challenges related to both national cultures and structure.

First consider culture. In the United States many professionals favor flexible work arrangements that enable them to transport work from the office to the home and work at times that best fit their other family commitments. Smaller proportions of workers in the United States prefer to restrict work to the office and maintain a rigid boundary between work and family roles. The opposite is true in India. Among Indian professional workers, long hours are understood as part of the job, but the preference is to keep office work at the office and not bring any work home. In that society, the preference (for most workers) is to keep work and family separated and confined, not integrated and overlapping (Poster & Prasad, 2005). These types of cultural dynamics present challenges to multinational employers intent on creating unified human resource policies and practices. Should the employer create a unique set of policies for employees in each country, or should it attempt to create a uniform set of policies modeled after the preferences that exist in a particular location? There are no easy answers.

Now consider structure. In the United States few regulations restrict employers from allowing workers to bring work home, and there are no limits on the number of hours employers can expect workers to labor. Workers are not entitled to vacation time by law, but many employers offer employees 2 or 3 weeks of vacation each year. In the European Union, by contrast, most workers are entitled to a month (and sometimes more) vacation per year, and employees have the right to refuse overtime work. If a multinational employer wanted to make employment standards consistent across its global operations, it would find legal (such as work time regulations and workplace inspection rules) and procedural hurdles (such as with unions) varying from society to society. In respect to work hours and vacation rights, the terms of employment in the United States would change remarkably if the European standards were adopted. Alternately, employers in the United States are more likely to offer some type of flexible work options than employers in France. In part this is because the French are more accepting of the government's involvement in family affairs, whereas Americans tend to look to employers to provide benefits. In addition, it is simply more difficult to alter work arrangements in France because of union resistance and the complexity of the legal system (Ollier-Malaterre, 2009). It can be challenging to establish one set of standards for all locations.

Some multinational companies are providing examples of ways to integrate flexibility into work. Consider, for example, the case of Merck, a global pharmaceutical company. In 2008 the company formalized its Global Flexibility Initiative Policy, which operates on assumptions that flexibility is good for its business and its employees. The policy has six tenets:

1. All covered employees are eligible to request a flexible work arrangement.

2. Managers approve or disapprove flexible work arrangement requests.

3. The manager and employee should discuss which options(s) is/are most appropriate based on the specific role responsibilities.

4. Occasional flexibility is encouraged in addition to flexible work arrangements as long as business needs are met.

5. This policy does not cover flexible work arrangements otherwise provided by law.

6. Flexible work arrangements may not be applicable for all roles.

When first formulating this policy, the goal was to create a means of helping the organization become more inclusive of women. The challenge was to formulate a policy that could accomplish this goal and be implementable across Merck's global operations, which required considering employee needs, business needs, and legal structures as they vary across societies. When the policy was implemented, some human resource officers responded with skepticism, wondering why a policy such as this needed to be implemented in their own locations, where these types of practices were

Global Work-Life Strategies in Multinational Corporations (MNCs)

Anne Bardoel

As a work-family scholar living in an era of phrases such as *we live in a global village* or *the world is getting smaller,* I have become increasingly interested in the issues faced by working women and men and their families from around the world in balancing their work and family lives. This natural curiosity was also stimulated by Jody Heymann's research as part of the Project on Global Working Families that specifically focused on understanding and improving the relationship between working conditions and family health and well-being globally. The difficulties of balancing work and family life are experienced all over the world, but in multinational corporations (MNCs) the effectiveness of the work-life policies is highly affected by local culture and national policies. So started my research journey a decade ago examining the role of global work-life strategies in MNCs.

Initially it was evident that our understanding of global work-life strategies lagged behind recognition by practitioners of its importance. With my colleague Helen De Cieri, we have conducted a number of interviews with senior HR and diversity managers in multinationals to find out who takes responsibility for work-life management. There are major challenges, particularly for MNCs seeking to operate in developing and growing markets, such as the large emerging markets of Brazil, Russia, India, and China. Corporate headquarter HR professionals need to have responsibility for formulating global policy, yet also need to be responsive to local concerns. For senior executives, responsibilities include endorsement of work-life initiatives and provision of adequate resourcing. Finally, HR practitioners must address the challenge of working with line managers and employees to build their competencies; training programs, advisory services, and resources that lead to work-life initiatives embedded in MNCs.

Anne Bardoel is an associate professor in the Department of Management, Monash University, Australia, and coauthor of "Global Work-Life Management in Multinational Corporations" in *International Human Resource Management* (Sage, 2011).

mandated by law. But those operating in other societies saw it as a significant change in the company's approach to managing its talent. In its first full year of implementation, over 1,000 requests for flexible work were approved, and the vast majority (80%) were from within the United States (Muse, 2011).

Summary

Many very good reasons can be provided to explain why companies should consider the impact that family obligations have on worker engagement. Taking these concerns into account can address a wide range of business-related issues—ranging from productivity and quality assurance to employee recruitment and retention. A goal is to increase employers' awareness of work-family connections, as well as help them identify effective strategies that correspond with the needs of their workforces. As more employers accept new time and place management practices as effective ways of organizing work, greater numbers of employees will have enhanced opportunity to move work around family, rather than the other way around. That a significant proportion of employers operate in decidedly family-unfriendly ways should not lead one to conclude that there is not a business case for responsive employment. It only indicates the need to recognize the limits of the business case to address work-family concerns and also the need to work with—and beyond—employer self-interest to catalyze change.

Useful Concepts

Business case. The recognition that work-family tensions can undermine business effectiveness and that addressing these tensions can enhance organizational functioning (Kossek & Fried, 2006).

Dual agenda. The perspective that family and employer interests are not adversarial, and both employers and families can benefit by reformulating the ways work is performed (Bailyn, Bookman, Harrington, & Kochan, 2006).

Flexible work arrangements. Job designs that enable workers to use discretion in respect to where, when, how much, or how long they will work (Golden, 2001b).

Formal availability. Programs or policies structured to be "on the books," which may or may not be considered usable in practice (Eaton, 2003).

Informal availability. Culturally based understandings that lend shape to the access and responses toward programs or policies (Eaton, 2003).

Organizational justice. The extent that fairness is evident in workplace practices and programs. Justice can be considered in respect to the ways resources are allocated, decision making processes, and interpersonal treatment (Trefalt, 2010).

Return on investment. A cost-benefit analysis that considers the expenditures involved in initiating a program and the positive results anticipated (Kelly et al., 2008).

Issues to Ponder

1. Suppose you work for a large manufacturing company of 1,000 employees that runs a single shift from 9:00 a.m. to 5:00 p.m. You read a study about the benefits of compressed work week schedules (4 days a week, 10 hours per day) and have advocated to your employer that the company should try a new schedule arrangement. Most of your coworkers agree that the alternate schedule would be good for their family lives. The owner expresses interest but says that his decision will be based primarily on economic concerns and that you should write up a cost-benefit report that considers the return on investment. What costs and benefits should be analyzed in the report you write? Which of these costs and benefits are quantifiable, and which are not?

2. Suppose a hospital introduces a new scheduling system in response to low work-family balance satisfaction among its employees (especially nurses). This new system operates on the basis of bidding for shifts (those who agree to work the least preferred shifts can receive higher compensation in return). The new system has more employees working shorter hours than before but also some employees work much longer hours than before. Fewer are working regular full-time shifts. Most of the employees (but not all) who work shorter hours are doing so because that is their preference, and most (but not all) of the workers who are laboring much longer hours are doing so because that is their preference. You need to assess the outcomes of this new system on hospital operations. What measures are critical to your evaluation of this change in scheduling practices?

3. Suppose that your employer provides, among other benefits and programs, the following: supplemental support for college tuition of employees' children, family health benefits, family leave to new parents, and funds to cover expenses involved in adopting children. Suppose also that you are never going to have children. Is this system unfair? Is there anything that your employer could do to make this system more equitable to employees such as yourself?

Mini Project

Select an employer you might consider working for and examine its human resources website for its work-life philosophy and specific policies and benefits. Look for items such as the following:

- Vacation policy
- Spousal hiring policy or resources
- Family leave policy
- Flexible work options
- Contributions to retirement plans or pensions
- College savings contributions
- Benefits for same-sex partners

5

Global Perspectives on the Work-Family Interface: International Comparative Analysis and Transnational Relationships

This chapter looks at global perspectives on the work-family interface and how these lenses can inform policy and practice. International comparative analyses can reveal strengths, limitations, and weaknesses in ways the work-family interface is organized. By considering other societies, this comparative approach expands the imagination of what can be done to reconcile institutional tensions and recognizes possible trade-offs in dismantling one type of approach in favor of another. Attention is then drawn to transnational connections and the ways family and work arrangements are interconnected across societies. This perspective reveals that arrangements in the United States are made possible, in part, by work-family arrangements elsewhere in the global economy. And by virtue of these connections, the ways that dominant nations in the global economy organize work and family commitments shape work and family roles in less developed economies. Oftentimes these connections allocate heavier risks and burdens to foreign-born care workers, who labor in service of other working families. As in previous chapters, the concern here is to identify points of tension in the work-family interface, as well as ways work and family institutions can operate synergistically.

International Comparative Analysis of Work and Family Relationships

One way of integrating a global focus on work and family is to compare societies against one another. This strategy of international comparative analysis is intended to understand the divergent ways that societies construct—and respond to—the work-family interface (Sweet, 2011). It should be no surprise that societies are remarkably varied in their reliance on different work-family arrangements. Societal-level practices can involve structuring rigid gender regimes in which men and women occupy distinct roles with little overlap, such as in Saudi Arabia. Societies can also configure generational ties to include extended kin networks, such as the care Greek children receive from grandmothers. And the structure of work-family arrangements varies from society to society, as reflected in various policies that might promote or discourage labor force attachment, regulate the terms of employment, or lend shape to supports provided to families. International comparative research, which focuses on the variations from one society to the next, reveals the relative successes (and failures) of different approaches to reconciling possible tensions (Gornick & Meyers, 2003). In its best form, aside from documenting societal variation, international comparative research reveals the factors that contribute to different societal outcomes, making it possible to understand, for example, the impact that specific efforts to address the work-family interface will likely produce.

It is tempting to present a particular society as a model for others to follow, one that exemplifies the laws and social programs that best resolve work-family tensions. If pressed to name such a place, many work-family advocates would direct attention to Sweden or some other Nordic society (as discussed in greater detail in this chapter) that offers generous family leave provisions to parents, extended vacations, shorter work hours, universal health care, expansive unemployment compensation, and a variety of other supports. Evidence shows that most outcomes of these family-supportive policies have been positive—especially when considering the interests of children, who live happier, safer, and healthier lives as a result. But as discussed later, these types of provisions are associated with significantly higher taxes and other downsides. And as the aging of countries like Sweden (and even more so Italy and Japan) increases the proportion of their population out of the labor force, revenue strains will inevitably result. Additionally, the regulatory structure in these societies (as compared to the United States) is less "business friendly," which some argue undermines their economic vitality. These types of observations suggest that there is a greater benefit to be gained by identifying the trade-offs from different societal strategies of

Work-Family Reconciliation Policy in Cross-National Perspective

Janet C. Gornick

In 1990, while completing my PhD in political economy and government with a concentration in social policy, I moved to Luxembourg to take a job with the Luxembourg Income Study, a small research center, now referred to as "LIS." The job entailed documenting social policies across a group of high-income countries. Those were the days before comparative social policy information was widely available in electronic form, so I spent months acquiring multi-country policy reports and travelling to various sites to gather country-specific policy information. As is often said, when we learn about "other" countries, often the most profound lessons concern our own. I was stunned to learn that the United States is an international laggard in social policy provision, and, as I would learn over the next many years, that is especially true with regard to work-family reconciliation policies—most especially policies that support or provide childcare, paid family leave, and the regulation of working time.

Since then, my research has concerned variation across countries—mostly high-income countries—in the provision of public policies that enable workers to balance their responsibilities on the job with their caregiving responsibilities at home. Much of my research assesses the ways in which policy design details enable or encourage gender-egalitarian divisions of labor in both paid and unpaid work. In several studies, I have used the "natural experiment" of cross-national policy variation to assess the effects of work-family policies on family economic well-being and on women's position in the labor market. I have made it a priority to make my research findings available and accessible to state and national policy makers across the United States, by writing policy briefs and participating in meetings in policy settings. I believe deeply that the United States must look abroad for work-family policy lessons, both positive and cautionary.

Janet C. Gornick is professor of political science and sociology at the Graduate Center/City University of New York and director of LIS, a cross-national data archive and research center in Luxembourg. She is coauthor of *Families That Work: Policies for Reconciling Parenthood and Employment* (Russell Sage Foundation Press, 2003) and *Gender Equality: Transforming Family Divisions of Labor* (Verso Press, 2009).

Cross-National Work-Family Research: State and Workplace Support

Laura den Dulk

My research focuses on the way national governments and organizations support workers who combine work and family life. Cross-national research shows us that the degree of public work-family provisions varies across countries. Within Europe, Scandinavian countries like Sweden and Finland offer the most generous policies, while state support in the U.K., the Netherlands, or Germany is more modest. Regarding workplace support, findings indicate that the public sector and large companies are taking the lead.

There are basically two arguments concerning this relationship between state support and employer practices. First, building on the institutional theory, public provisions indicate a strong government commitment to the combination of work and family life and may create normative and coercive pressure on organizations to develop additional support. Hence, the more state support in a country for the combination of work and family life, the more work-family support in organizations. Alternately, economic theory suggests that the presence of public policies makes it less likely for employers to develop their own additional provisions. Rather it is the absence of public policy that stimulates organizations to develop provisions to have a competitive advantage over other employers in the recruitment and retention of talented workers. So far, evidence from cross-national research points toward a positive relation between state and workplace support, although the strength of the relation varies across types of organizations.

Variation between organizations has implications for equality of access to work-family support. If state support is low, workers become more dependent on organizational provisions, and there is more inequality in access. My research shows that a positive relation between state and organizational support can ensure more equality of access and can, at the same time, stimulate organizations to develop facilities that suit the specific needs of both the organization and the employees.

Laura den Dulk is an associate professor at the Department of Public Administration, Erasmus University Rotterdam, the Netherlands, and coauthor of *Work-Life Balance Support in the Public Sector in Europe* (Roppa, 2012).

managing work-family relationships, rather than assuming an unequivocal superiority of one country's solutions over approaches adopted elsewhere.

Culture plays a major role in the ways policies are defined and implemented. If one were to argue that Sweden's policies are superior, there is little assurance that these policies stand a chance of making it through the legislative process in the United States. In fact, there is ample evidence to suggest that passage of comparable entitlements or regulations is unlikely given that concerns such as paid family leave, work hour laws, and access to childcare services are not current agenda items of the U.S. Congress. An additional barrier is that the U.S. system itself imposes significant hurdles in establishing bold new policy initiatives, as any legislation proposed must be passed within a limited time frame or be pushed to the back of the table (Feldblum & Appleberry, 2006). And with the antitax climate in the United States, even if a case were made for this legislation, it is not evident that sufficient support among the American public can be generated. These observations reveal that ameliorating work-family conflict is much more complicated than simply identifying the best policies from a menu of choices.

Intersections of Culture and Policy: National Approaches to Support Care Work

Many analysts have observed remarkable differences between the ways that the United States approaches the work-family interface as compared to other advanced economies, noting in particular the limited scale and scope of publicly financed resources available to support working families. Among the important differences are family leave policies, financial supports for engagement in care work, and resources that facilitate parental integration in the labor force. By comparing societies, it is evident that cultural values play a significant role not only in the way policies are constructed, but also how they are implemented and used.

Family Leave

Family leave policies enable workers to take time away from their jobs to provide care in service of other family members. These policies can differ in a number of respects, including duration, compensation, and eligibility. As Exhibit 5.1 shows, the extent of leave varies widely among societies. Sweden, Norway, Denmark, and the United Kingdom offer the most generous leave programs, enabling new parents to take as much as 52 to 64 weeks of paid leave from their jobs. In contrast, the United States provides a much shorter

Work and Family in the Neoliberal Caribbean

Carla Freeman

I began examining the complexities of work and family in the Caribbean 20 years ago with a focus on new global industries settling in the region in search of cheap labor. In contrast to laboring in the cane fields, hotels, or blue-collar assembly jobs, the focus was on "pink collar" informatics, information processing and data entry work setting the stage for the current "outsourcing" boom in India and elsewhere. In much of Asia and Latin America, women's entry into new global industries represented a radical transformation, especially when men were increasingly without jobs and women were traditionally expected to maintain the domestic sphere. In the Caribbean, by contrast, women's history of labor participation and their strong role as mothers *and* workers led them to reject rules that prevailed in global industries, such as strict policies against pregnancy and rigid definitions of the ideal worker as young, single, childless, and feminine.

In my recent research I trace a new culture of entrepreneurialism in the Caribbean encompassing both a growing interest in self-employment and self-making more generally. Here, the relationships between "work" and "nonwork"—leisure, family, intimate relationships—have become blurry. Across the public-private divide, they hinge upon emotional or "affective" labor oriented toward the body and "the self" (therapeutic services, spiritual practices, new modes of consumption, new expressions of "partnership marriage" and parenting, new concepts of "the couple," "the child," and "quality time") that appear deceptively familiar to a Euro-American eye. Again, my analysis shows that despite similarities in form, their meanings are new and distinctive to the cultural context in which they emerge. The case of work-family relationships in the Caribbean reveals that concepts such as "labor" and "middle class" are not generic but must be interpreted through the particular contours of culture, gender, and race.

Carla Freeman is Winship Distinguished Research Professor of Anthropology and Women's Studies at Emory University and author of *High Tech and High Heels in the Global Economy: Women, Work, and Pink-Collar Identities in the Caribbean* (Duke University Press, 2000) and *Enterprising Selves: Neoliberalism, Respectability, and the Making of a Caribbean Middle Class* (Duke University Press, forthcoming).

leave entitlement. Under the Family Medical Leave Act, the entitlement is 12 weeks of unpaid absence, but this is restricted to full-time workers who have worked for their employer for at least one year. This policy has had little impact on the lives of lower-income workers, who cannot afford to be without an income even if they are eligible for leave.

While extended paid family leave fosters opportunity to provide quality care, some unintended consequences can result. One concern is that gender inequality in Nordic countries (where family leave options are most generous) tends to be higher than in the United States. In other words, women in the United States have a greater chance of reaching higher-level managerial positions than women in Sweden, and they also have a greater chance of earning higher incomes (Mandel, 2009; Mandel & Semyonov, 2006). However, it is important to note that the impact of family leave on gender inequality is primarily experienced by members of the middle and upper-middle classes in Nordic countries, not by members of the lower classes (Mandel, 2011). This suggests that the more generous leave policies have introduced the unintended consequence of creating a disincentive to hire women for demanding positions, out of concern that they will be less than dependable employees over the long term. So while family leave entitlements can help solve the problem of time strains and care needs, when not intentionally structured to encourage use by men, they also tend to reinforce gendered social arrangements.

Because paid family leave entitlements are almost exclusively used by women, some countries have introduced "father quotas" or "daddy months" in order to motivate men to take leave as well. These are nontransferrable entitlements set aside for the spouse or partner who has not already taken the primary leave to which a couple may be entitled. For example, in Iceland mothers and fathers are each entitled to 3 months of paid leave, with an additional month of paid leave that they can allocate to either partner as they wish. Evidence indicates that additional motivators (such as these types of "use it or lose it" policies) are needed to move men temporarily out of the labor force and into care work in the home (Haas & Rostgaard, 2011). Family leave options that promote paternal care can also have an enduring impact on leveling differences in gender role behavior in other ways, such as the division of household work (Kotsadam & Finseraas, 2011). However, family leave policies are not always introduced with a goal of creating or enhancing gender equality. In the case of the Netherlands, for example, the "one and a half workers" family structure is a normative arrangement, with husbands working full-time jobs and wives working part time (Peters, den Dulk, & van der Lippe, 2009). In this society, gender imbalances in leave-taking are not viewed as a major societal concern, nor are gendered career paths.

Exhibit 5.1   Family Leave Entitlements in Developed Countries

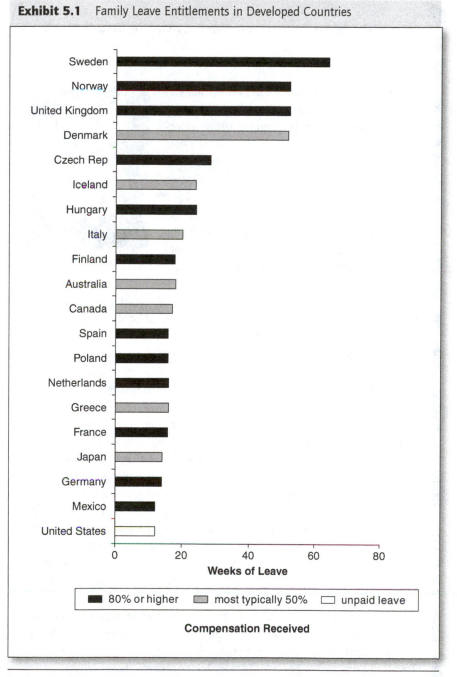

Source: United Nations Statistics and Indicators on Women and Men (2011)

Studying Fathers on the Frontier in Sweden

Linda Haas

While taking courses in Scandinavian studies in graduate school, I discovered that Swedish policy makers were the first in the world in 1968 to challenge the traditional gendered division of labor, where fathers are responsible for earning and mothers are responsible for caregiving. Women and men were declared to have the same rights and responsibilities to have a job and to care for home and children. This goal, today labeled "the dual-breadwinner/dual-caregiver family model," is deeply rooted in political and popular culture.

In 1975, I made my first trip to Sweden and discovered that only one year before Sweden had become the first nation to offer paid parental leave to fathers. Today, fathers have 2 nontransferable months of highly paid leave, along with 9 months to share with partners. I decided to study leave policy to see if it encourages couples to share childcare, a development I was convinced was necessary for women's equal employment opportunity in the labor market. Parental leave for fathers challenges gendered assumptions about women's unique role as caregivers and bestows social and monetary value to caregiving.

My research on couples revealed that fathers were interested in sharing childcare, experienced benefits from leavetaking, and that leavetaking increased couples' sharing of childcare. (See *Equal Parenthood and Social Policy*, SUNY Press, 1992.) However, men reported workplaces were not supportive of their leavetaking. Consequently, in recent years my research has focused on how the gendered structure and culture of work organizations reinforces the traditional division of family labor. Companies have been slow to support men as caregivers, but younger men expecting to combine employment with family life are pushing for change. Companies are beginning to report that support for fathers contributes not just to their public image but also to their bottom line, since caregiving fathers are more productive at work.

Linda Haas is professor of sociology and adjunct professor of women's studies at Indiana University-Purdue University, Indianapolis, and coauthor with C. Philip Hwang of "Is Fatherhood Becoming More Visible at Work?—Trends in Corporate Support for Fathers Taking Parental Leave in Sweden" in *Fathering* 7:303–21 (2009).

Financial Supports for Care Work

Paid family leave is one means of compensating care work performed by family members. However, compensation (when available) is contingent on prior labor force attachment. Most societies have also developed means of compensating nonfamilial care work, but the level and range of resources vary widely. For example, in the United States, Medicare provides financial assistance to meet the medical needs of the elderly. Through this program, older citizens are able to purchase care, such as that which might be provided by home care workers. However, the amount of funds allocated is often insufficient to cover all needed expenses, and related policies in the United States shape the quality of care available. For example, home care aids (who made on average $9.70 per hour in 2010) are exempt from some protections in the Fair Labor Standards Act and as a consequence labor without the right to overtime pay that most other hourly wage workers are entitled to receive (Greenhouse, 2011). The low wages received by these workers directly affects the quality of the services that can be expected.

In contrast, consider the system used in the Netherlands, where "personal budgets" are used to provide compensation for the care of the elderly (and other needy family members). This system involves allocating money directly to the care recipient (e.g., the elderly individual), funds that she or he can use to purchase assistance. Because care recipients have discretion to hire any individual of their own choosing, most elect to employ other family members, which compensates these family members for the care work they perform. This approach to valuing care stands in stark contrast to the U.S. model, where family members are prohibited from being directly compensated from sources such as Medicare. However, critics of the Dutch system note that it may undermine the quality of care, as it reduces the ability of professional groups to manage and regulate the standards under which care work is performed (Kremer, 2006).

Entitlements that Facilitate Integration in the Paid Labor Force

An alternate approach to supporting care work is to move it away from the family sphere and into the public domain. This can be achieved by, for example, providing universal access to high-quality childcare or elder care programs. These types of programs can be seen in places such as Finland and France, which differ from the United States and its reliance on privately negotiated care arrangements and heavy dependence on care provided directly by family members.

The access to, and use of, childcare centers provides an interesting illustration of how culture and structure intertwine. In France, for example, all parents have the option to put children in publicly funded childcare centers, and the vast majority of parents take advantage of this resource. Unlike in the United States, staff members in these centers are highly trained and well compensated, which in turn enhances the quality of care received. The French do not view this care as being "cold" in comparison to the "warm" care that might be provided in the home. Instead, the use of public childcare centers is viewed very favorably (Pfau-Effinger, 2004). In contrast to the United States, childcare is widely available and affordable in France, which significantly decreases work-family strains.

One recent study considered what happens when two cultures are presented with the same options for publicly supported childcare. Even though Germany is united today, the legacy of the Cold War created significant cultural differences that remain among Germans today, depending on whether they live in the East or the West. Although all Germans have access to the same types of social programs throughout the country, Western German women are much more likely to work part time than Eastern German women and do so because they see direct care as a responsibility to their family. They also are less likely to place their children in care centers (Pfau-Effinger & Smidt, 2011). Apparently even if state-supported childcare centers alleviate care concerns, they will not be met with the same reaction in all societies, and in some cultures this approach to reconciling work with family will be viewed as less than ideal.

When societies enhance the availability of economic resources to purchase care, they can make a substantial impact on both the quality of care received and the way it is provided. But again, culture plays a significant role. Consider Japan, with its tradition of familial care for the elderly (Kumagai, 1984). After the passage of the Long Term Care Insurance Act of 2000, which provides funds for elder care services, the amount of time daughters spent caring for their aging parents significantly declined. But even with these resources, responsibility for family care is still primarily allocated to daughters and daughters-in-law (Lee, 2010). And consistent with traditional Japanese culture and its reliance on family care, the norm is to use these funds to bring care workers into the home, rather than to move the elderly into outside institutions (Soma & Yamashita, 2011).

In the United States, care work is largely considered a private family concern, and for that reason there has not been a concerted push toward institutionalizing childcare or elder care outside of the home. Middle- and upper-income families can receive a tax deduction for childcare expenses, which in effect subsidizes their budgets, but families face significant challenges in locating quality, affordable care providers. While some low-income families have access to childcare services through the program Head Start, the availability and quality of these services is uneven. As a consequence, until children reach school age, working parents in the United States face greater difficulties in securing care as compared to many other societies.

In the United States, considerable attention has been directed to increasing labor force attachment and far less so to institutionalizing means of providing care outside the family, creating and exacerbating strains on families. As one example, consider the reformulation of welfare policy in the United States. Currently, the primary income subsidy for poor families is through the program Temporary Assistance to Needy Families (TANF). This program, introduced through the 1996 Personal Responsibility and Work Opportunity Reconciliation Act, replaced an older welfare system, Aid to Families with Dependent Children (AFCD), by imposing limitations on the receipt of welfare benefits to a lifetime maximum of 5 years and a work expectation for nearly all recipients (including those with young children). This legislation was intended to motivate individuals to be self-reliant and to reduce welfare dependency. However, the legislation did not effectively address related concerns that stem from imposing work expectations on welfare recipients, such as increasing access to childcare services. As a consequence of TANF, as parents left their homes to engage in low-wage work, children in poor families were exposed to substantial new risks, and their parents were subjected to increased strain and worry (Crouter & Booth, 2004). Two obvious ways of addressing these concerns would be to either improve the wages provided in the types of jobs that TANF recipients enter or increase the availability and affordability of childcare centers. Neither concern has been a national priority in the past decade.

There is remarkable variation in the ways different societies approach the work-family interface, and this variation is a product of both structure and culture. Recognizing that values give shape to policy is an important contribution of cross-national research on work and family. International comparative research also indicates that when resources are made available, it should be expected that preexisting cultural attitudes shape who uses them and how. It should not be assumed that "what works there will work here." At the same time, cross-national research also demonstrates the merits of alternate ways of constructing the work-family interface, and as discussed shortly, ample evidence indicates that the United States has not developed the most effective or equitable strategy of doing so.

Three Societal-Level Approaches to Reconciling Work-Family Strains

How are we to make sense of such varied national approaches to reconciling work with family? While no society is "pure" in its approach, it is apparent that different societies tend to stress different solutions. In considering these variations, three overarching approaches to formulating national work-family policies are identifiable. Each approach, while potentially alleviating tensions, operates on a different logic and creates different types of consequences.

Approach 1: Emancipate Caregivers from the Need to Work Outside the Home

One possible means of reconciling time strains and care needs is for societies to develop mechanisms that enable people to exit the paid labor force. The overarching strategy, within this framework, is to free time from work, and this can be done in a variety of ways, including discouraging overwork, expanding options for paid leave, providing "personal budgets" to compensate caregivers, or by otherwise financially compensating the care provided within families. A key challenge in advancing this approach is placing an economic value on care work performed by family members. This approach is evident in Nordic countries such as Sweden and Norway.

Approach 2: Emancipate Workers from Caregiving

An alternate national approach to alleviating work-family strain is to relieve the need for workers to attend to concerns in the home. The logic in this strategy is to enable family members to worry less about each other's care needs by institutionalizing care services through supports such as universal childcare, access to elder care services, provision of afterschool activities, and access to other service providers. While some of these services might be considered "cold" in comparison to the "warm" care received within families, these perceptions are not universally shared across cultures. Addressing both the availability and quality of services is critical to maximizing the effectiveness of this strategy. This approach is evident in France and Germany.

Approach 3: Provide Dual Supports

A third approach—that of providing dual supports—considers mechanisms that enable caregivers to remain within the labor force and for workers to provide care. As is evident in the first two approaches, there are trade-offs involved in directing people's attention to either the workforce or home, as most men and women wish to be engaged in both worlds. And for that reason, even in societies that make emancipation from one domain or the other possible, there is high involvement in both work and family spheres. In the United States, attachment to *both* work and family is not simply a consequence of financial need; it also is the result of personal preferences. Dual supports can be designed and implemented to make this possible.

Regulations, those that influence the terms under which labor occurs, are one means of providing dual supports. For example, because the United States has no effective work hour regulations (other than overtime pay for nonexempt workers), far greater proportions of the labor force work far longer hours than they prefer. And because most part-time jobs are excluded from protections and benefits packages, there are penalties for scaling back on work (Sweet & Meiksins, 2012). In contrast, Western European nations such as the United Kingdom have instituted rights to request reduced work hours for a variety of situations, including a gradual return to work, parental leave on a part-time basis, or (for older workers) reduced hours while receiving a partial pension (Hegewisch & Gornick, 2008). Expanding options to labor less, but still work under reasonably attractive terms, can ease strain on fulfillment of work and family roles.

Dual supports also can be created within neighborhoods and communities, enhancing the capacity of people to labor with fewer distractions from the home. For example, provision of resources needed to transform unsafe neighborhoods into safer environments can make a world of difference in reducing the need for parents to be with their children in the afterschool hours and limiting the negative consequences if they are not (Bookman, 2004; Booth & Crouter, 2000). The quality of neighborhood resources, including access to affordable housing, recreational opportunities, and quality schools, is of considerable importance in creating family-friendly communities (Sweet, Swisher, & Moen, 2005; Swisher, Sweet, & Moen, 2004).

The argument in favor of dual supports is not an argument against the other two approaches. In fact, it is a hybrid approach that selects and adapts means of expanding resources, as well as curtailing demands, in both the work and family spheres. To the extent that paid leave and publicly supported childcare and elder care are included in the formulation, dual supports can be part of an agenda to emancipate workers from some care obligations. The provision of dual supports also can be viewed as a quality-of-life issue, which moves discourse away from it being an accommodation for women and toward it being in service of workers in general. For these reasons, this may be the most viable strategy of advancing family-responsive policies that resonate with dominant cultural values in the United States.

Family Well-Being in International Comparative Perspective

Much of what we know about international variation in work-family policies and their outcomes is restricted to societies with advanced economies as measured by the Organization for Economic and Cooperative Development (OECD). This leaves outside of the analysis underdeveloped and emerging economies, where work and family challenges can be even greater (Heymann, Earle, & Hanchate, 2004). Nonetheless, much can be learned by comparing these more affluent societies against one another in respect to some basic standards of family well-being.

Focusing first on children, consider data presented in the United Nations report "Child Poverty in Perspective: An Overview of Child Well-Being in Rich Countries" (UNICEF, 2007). This report considers a variety of indicators concerning how well children are performing in different societies and the quality of their lives. Included in the analysis are the following:

- Material well-being (i.e., relative poverty, children in households without an employed adult, material deprivation)
- Health and safety (i.e., health up to age 1, access to preventative health services, accidental death rates)
- Educational well-being (i.e., reading and math literacy achievements, percentage enrolled in school)
- Family and peer relationships (i.e., percentage living with single parents, percentage eating main meal of the day with parents more than once per week, percentage of children reporting that parents spend time "just talking" to them, percentage reporting that peers are "kind and helpful")
- Behaviors and risks (i.e., percentage who eat healthful foods, percentage who exercise, drinking and smoking behaviors, risky sexual activity, engagement or victimization in violence)
- Subjective well-being (i.e., percentage reporting health as favorable, percentage "liking school a lot," percentage reporting positively about their personal well-being)

Exhibit 5.2 shows the relative rankings of all 21 countries assessed, with 1 being the most favorable rank and 21 the least favorable. Notice that Nordic countries tend to rank high on most of the well-being dimensions. What these countries share in common are numerous entitlements, such as those that provide for extensive family leave and universal health care. In contrast, far fewer supports exist in countries ranked at the low end of the report, including Australia, Hungary, the United States, and the United Kingdom. These findings support the conclusion that the ways a society elects to manage work-family arrangements have a significant impact on personal well-being.

Exhibit 5.2 Summary Rankings of Child Well-Being in Developed Economies

Dimensions of Child Well Being	Average Ranking Position	Material Well-Being	Health and Safety	Educational Well-Being	Family and Peer Relationships	Behaviors and Risks	Subjective Well-Being
Netherlands	4.2	10	2	6	3	3	1
Sweden	5.0	1	1	5	15	1	7
Denmark	7.2	4	4	8	9	6	12
Finland	7.5	3	3	4	17	7	11
Spain	8.0	12	6	15	8	5	2
Switzerland	8.3	5	9	14	4	12	6
Norway	8.7	2	8	11	10	13	8
Italy	10.0	14	5	20	1	10	10
Ireland	10.2	19	19	7	7	4	5
Belgium	10.7	7	16	1	5	19	16
Germany	11.2	13	11	10	13	11	9
Greece	11.8	15	18	16	11	8	3
Canada	11.8	6	13	2	18	17	15
Poland	12.3	21	15	3	14	2	19
Czech Republic	12.5	11	10	9	19	9	17
France	13.0	9	7	18	12	14	18
Portugal	13.7	16	14	21	2	15	14
Austria	13.8	8	20	19	16	16	4
Hungary	14.5	20	17	13	6	18	13
United States	18.0	17	21	12	20	20	-
United Kingdom	18.2	18	12	17	21	21	20

Note: Darker shades indicate lower rankings on each dimension.

Source: UNICEF. 2007. "Child Poverty in Perspective: An Overview of Child Well-Being in Rich Countries." United Nations Children's Fund. Florence, Italy.

In the United States risks associated with aging are largely carried as private affairs, as existing public supports provided by Medicare, Medicaid, and Social Security Insurance leave significant gaps in coverage (Bookman & Kimbrel, 2011). Financial comfort in later life for most workers hinges on personal decisions (and the capacity) to invest portions of earnings into private retirement accounts such as 401(k)s. Because community-based care options are commonly unavailable or out of reach for the frail elderly in the United States, many end up warehoused in less desirable facilities, alone or in the care of time- and financially-strapped children. These family caregivers comprise a "shadow workforce" in the geriatric health care system and seldom receive compensation for their efforts. In contrast, Denmark has instituted a number of state-supported community resources available to the frail elderly. As a consequence, nursing home placement in Denmark is half the rate of that in the United States, and the elderly are far more likely to live independent from their children than in the United States. In other words, by mobilizing community care resources for the needs of the elderly, Denmark relieved strains on adult children (who would more likely be providing care to aging parents in the United States), as well as enhanced the quality of life for the elderly in their later years (Stuart & Hansen, 2006).

Comparisons across societies reveal not only variation in the approaches to reconciling work with family, but also the consequences of these approaches. The United States stands apart in the volume of potential resources to help ease the problems associated with caregiving, and its failure to effectively mobilize these resources. As compared to benchmarks of personal and family well-being established in other societies, a much wider gap separates current conditions from what is achievable.

Transnational Concerns

On May 12, 2008, the United States Immigration and Naturalization Service (INS) conducted its single largest employer raid in its efforts to round up suspected illegal immigrants. Their focus was Agriprocessors, a kosher slaughterhouse in Postville, Iowa, a company with a poor record of compliance with labor and environmental regulations. A month in advance of the raid, the INS secured a compound to process detainees and hired interpreters to perform translations. Most of the 389 undocumented workers (nearly half of the company's workforce) were immigrants from two desperately poor communities in Guatemala. They had come to the United States to work—14 to 17 hours per day for $7.25 per hour in abusive conditions—in order to send money back to their families. To do so, some walked hundreds of miles, and others paid as much as $7,000 to secure entry across the border. Some brought their families with them. In the day following the raid, 1 in 3 children were absent from school, making evident the large number of illegal immigrant families in Postville. When these workers lost their jobs, their families—those at home in Guatemala and those who remained in the United States—were left in debt and without income.

In order to start work at Agriprocessors, the illiterate workers were instructed to enter random social security numbers, and no background checks were performed by their employer. Few, if any, knew what social security numbers were for or understood this as an illegal activity, but all understood that they had illegally entered the United States. At the trial, defense lawyers advised them to plead guilty to "knowingly using a false social security number," because a not-guilty plea would have likely resulted in a minimum of a 6-month trial wait in jail and a 2-year confinement thereafter for more serious charges. At their sentencing, when led to the court in chains and without precisely understanding the charges leveled against them, all of the workers accepted the plea agreement of 5 months in prison followed by immediate deportation. Many wept. When provided the opportunity, few offered comment to the court, but one defendant said, "Your honor, you know that we are here because of the need of our families. I beg that you find it in your heart to send us home before too long because we have a responsibility to our children, to give them an education, clothing, shelter, and food." One judge, who felt great sympathy, but who was also bound by INS directives that provided no opportunity for leniency, responded in his sentencing, "I don't doubt for a moment that you are good, hardworking people who have done what you did to help your families. Unfortunately for you, you committed a violation of a federal law" (Camayd-Freixas, 2008; Preston, 2008).

Half a world away, workers at Foxconn Technology Group in Shenzen, China, assemble electronics (such as iPads, iPhones, and computers) for American consumers. Many of these workers labor with other family members and also send money home to their relatives who reside in poor communities in rural China. Work conditions at Foxconn are hazardous and grueling, as workers can be expected to assemble as many as 1,600 hard drives per day. Shifts are long—11-hour days, 7 days a week, are common—and are far beyond what is permissible by Chinese law. For their efforts, workers earn about $1 per hour, or about $300 per month. They sleep in packed dormitories, commonly sharing rooms with nine other workers, and workplace stress is very high. On January 23, 2010, one of those workers, Ma Xiangqian, leapt to his death from his room in a high-rise dormitory, a path taken by others as well. In response, the company has installed nets to catch future would-be jumpers. Ma Xiangqian's father sought compensation from Foxconn, explaining, "He was my only son . . . only sons are very important in the countryside. What am I to do?" Only after much publicity about employee suicides, aversive conditions, and an explosion that killed 4 workers and seriously injured 18 others has the Apple corporation taken more seriously the need to monitor the labor practices of its direct suppliers. However, labor conditions in factories further up the supply chain, those that provide parts for Foxconn to assemble, remain largely unexamined by the company (Barboza, 2010a, 2010b; Duhigg & Barboza, 2012).

These illustrations reveal *transnational relationships*—connections among societies—that give shape to the work-family interface. For many workers, the nature of their jobs and family lives is influenced by global concerns stemming from production processes and labor flows that extend across national borders. Families are affected by the ways corporations structure their supply chains and recruit their labor, as well as by a variety of other transnational political, economic, and military policies that shape environmental conditions, domestic economies, trade policies, and immigration opportunities (and hazards). And for multinational corporations interested in establishing work-family policy directives, unique challenges emerge in satisfying the varied cultural and regulatory arrangements within the multiple societies in which they operate. These concerns are complicated, and the goal here is to simply identify transnational dynamics as a major contributor to both the challenges and successes of harmonizing work and family.

Transnational Families

While families are conventionally conceived as kin that share the same residence, in the global economy substantial proportions of families are separated not only by living quarters, but also by national borders. These transnational families survive by relying on one or more members to earn income abroad while others provide care in their country of origin (Zontini, 2007). In the United States many parents labor as undocumented workers in the agricultural and food processing sectors (but also in other industries), where as many as 1 in 7 workers are illegal immigrants (Broder, 2006). While some immigrants bring their families with them to the United States (raising questions about the rights and legal status of their children), others labor thousands of miles from families and send money home. Other immigrants in the United States, such as those who migrate from Europe and Asia, more commonly come through legal paths and are much more likely to be employed in higher-end jobs. And the United States is not unique in

Common Ground Around the World: The Lives of Working Families

Jody Heymann

As we spoke in Tegucigalpa, Gabriela cuddled her daughter in the barren shack that was her home. Childcare was not publicly provided in Honduras, and with the income she earned as a widowed single mother she could not pay for private care. Gabriela had started a new full-time job in a factory. Over the summer, Gabriela's 10-year-old sister had been caring for her 19-month-old, but the school year was about to start, and Gabriella would have to choose between leaving the toddler home alone and asking her young sister to leave school to care for her. Half a world away, Phuong's life in Ho Chi Minh City shared the need to balance caring for her young children and earning the income to feed, clothe, and educate them. Like Gabriela, she worked in a factory and could not be at home with them during the day. But in her case, publicly provided childcare was available, and it made all the difference.

At the beginning stages of my research on global working families, many colleagues expressed their doubts. Could families around the world really have much in common? After carrying out thousands of interviews in every region, together with an international team, it became clear that the commonalities were overwhelming. Working parents taught us about the daily challenges they faced as they sought to meet their children's needs from infancy through adolescence; countries across geography and income levels taught us that solutions to these challenges were possible and economically viable.

Finding solutions to balancing work and family is a keystone to addressing poverty and gender equity. I hope you will join us in these efforts—or find your own journey that will matter deeply to the lives of others as well as your own.

Jody Heymann is the founding director of the Institute for Health and Social Policy and author of *Forgotten Families: Ending the Growing Crisis Confronting Children and Working Parents in the Global Economy* (Oxford University Press, 2006) and *Raising the Global Floor: Dismantling the Myth That We Can't Afford Good Working Conditions for Everyone* (Stanford University Press, 2010).

its reliance on transnational families. In Dubai, for example, one can find Indian immigrants working in construction and Filipina and Sri Lankan immigrants working as domestic servants. In these societies immigrant workers are not permitted to purchase property, and their status as guests has an implicit understanding that transnational family members will not pursue or obtain the rights of native-born citizens. While suffering the burden of distance from kin, the incomes these earners receive are far higher than those obtainable in their countries of origin.

As increasing numbers of family members are separated by distance, a growing concern is the quality of care that children and aging parents receive when adult family members go abroad to find work. One way of understanding this concern is to consider the ways care—provided in both the developed and developing economies—is linked through "nanny chains"(Hochschild, 2000). One link in this chain is the need of families in the United States (and elsewhere) who lack time to provide hands-on care for their own children or aging parents. The low-cost care obtained from illegal immigrants fills this resource gap. It also connects more affluent families to nannies drawn from throughout the global system, women who migrate in search of work because economic opportunity in their own communities is so limited. But as these nannies serve the needs of wealthier families, they create a deficit in their own children's care. Although discomforting to acknowledge, the success that some women experience in advanced economies is made possible through the exploitation of women in developing economies (Mohanty, 2003). At its core, the nanny chain stems from a failure to value care work, the limited options available to workers employed in higher-wage work, and the financial desperation of workers who have few options other than to leave their families in search of work abroad.

Not all transnational families experience the challenges of those in the lower tiers of the economy. The growth in the reach of multinational corporations has led to the creation of new classes of highly valued international workers, including transnational managers. Much of the work performed by these employees occurs outside of their home country, but their roots largely remain back in their countries of origin. Most of these managers are men, and most have spouses and children. While some transnational managers bring their families with them, for many others the overseas assignment involves living apart for considerable periods of time. As a consequence, these workers experience some of the strains common to other transnational workers. However, it is important to note that access to technology and travel resources helps ease these strains. Transnational managers experience a mixed bag of positives and negatives from their global

Work-Family Issues on International Assignments

Mila Lazarova

A key theme in my research is enhancing understanding of how to make international assignments successful for both people and organizations. Families present a key source of support, but they can also present barriers to international mobility. Family issues are among the top reasons why assignments are turned down and remain a source of many negative experiences, mainly stemming from adjustment difficulties of family members.

In a recent collaboration with Mina Westman and Margaret Shaffer, I examine how the work and family spheres interact to produce positive work and family experiences. We distinguish between two important processes: *spillover* (the idea that one sphere of life can affect the other sphere) and *crossover* (the recognition that how one's partner feels about work and family can affect how the other partner feels about work and family). Crossover is critically important to understand in an expatriation context, as international relocation causes loss of support from extended family and friends, and expatriates and accompanying family members become more dependent on one another. Past research has tended to emphasize negative crossover from the expatriate partner to the expatriate, but we highlight that positive synergy between partners is equally likely and point out that it is not only partners that can influence expatriates but also expatriates that can influence partners. We also make the argument that to assess whether an assignment was successful, we must consider not just job performance but also "family performance." While some colleagues have questioned the label "performance" in the family domain, we strongly believe that we must account in some way for how people meet their family-related obligations and expectations and the extent to which this performance is influenced by what happens in the work domain. Our current work is designed to enhance this line of research.

Mila Lazarova is an associate professor of international business at the Beedie School of Business and director of the Centre for Global Workforce Strategy at Simon Fraser University, Vancouver, Canada. She is author of (with coauthors Mina Westman and Margaret Shaffer) "Elucidating the Positive Side of the Work-Family Interface on International Assignments: A Model of Expatriate Work and Family Performance" in *Academy of Management Review, 35*(1): 93–117 (2010).

assignments. For example, these workers and their families have opportunities to interact with different cultures and experience the enrichment from these encounters. But for others, job demands take a toll. One of the primary reasons why transnational managers shift to other assignments is because of the desire for stability in their family lives, which can be complicated by their job demands (Caligiuri & Lazarova, 2005).

In some ways globalization has been a boon to families, as many indicators (health, literacy, life expectancy) reveal that life quality is increasing (World Health Organization, 2010). However, the gaps that separate wealthier societies from most disadvantaged societies are not closing (Milanovic, 2005). In addition, the strains imposed on families are uneven, and gaping chasms exist between families at the low end of the economy in developing countries and those in the upper ends of developed societies. A transnational focus brings into sharp relief how families—those with privilege and those without—are connected to one another through complex exchanges of both care and commodities in the global economy. Few people wish to live apart from their families for extended periods of time, and yet the global economy appears to be increasing this structural arrangement. If a goal is to increase family cohesion, this will require rethinking ways of expanding economic opportunities in developing economies, and it may require some sacrifices on the part of families in developed economies (Isaksen, Devi, & Hochschild, 2008).

Summary

International comparative and transnational perspectives decenter understandings of the work-family interface by enabling one to see how other societies address relevant concerns, as well as how work-family connections are formed between societies. The structure of policies varies greatly in respect to the amount of resources allocated to both the work and family spheres, the ways resources are allocated, and the extent that work-family concerns are considered societal concerns. And cultural values play a significant role in determining both the shape of policy and the extent that specific policy initiatives are supported or resisted. While work-family concerns are now part of the public discussion in the United States, the extent of supports offered here are, on the whole, much more modest than those offered in other comparable economies. Evidence, based on international comparative analysis of personal and family well-being, indicates that the United States fails to sufficiently capitalize on its fullest potential. And some successes of American working families are achieved at the expense of families abroad. All of this indicates a need to restructure work, family, and work-family policies.

Useful Concepts

Daddy month(s). Parental leave restricted to a spouse or partner who has not already used the otherwise available leave entitlements (Haas & Rostgaard, 2011).

Dual supports. Provisions that enhance the prospect of maintaining an attachment to the labor force while simultaneously offering opportunities to provide care.

Family leave. "Family leave allows employees to take time off from work to care for their families, deal with an emergency, or recuperate from a serious illness with a guaranteed job when they return" (Paid Family Leave Coalition, 2001).

Family Medical Leave Act. "The FMLA entitles eligible employees of covered employers to take unpaid, job-protected leave for specified family and medical reasons with continuation of group health insurance coverage under the same terms and conditions as if the employee had not taken leave. Eligible employees are entitled to:

- Twelve workweeks of leave in a 12-month period for:
  o the birth of a child and to care for the newborn child within one year of birth;
  o the placement with the employee of a child for adoption or foster care and to care for the newly placed child within one year of placement;
  o care for the employee's spouse, child, or parent who has a serious health condition;
  o a serious health condition that makes the employee unable to perform the essential functions of his or her job;
  o any qualifying exigency arising out of the fact that the employee's spouse, son, daughter, or parent is a covered military member on "covered active duty;" *or*

- Twenty-six workweeks of leave during a single 12-month period to care for a covered servicemember with a serious injury or illness if the eligible employee is the servicemember's spouse, son, daughter, parent, or next of kin (military caregiver leave)." (U.S. Department of Labor, 2012)

Nanny chains. Connections that tie the care needs of families in advanced economies to the services provided by care workers from less developed economies (Hochschild, 1999).

Transnational families. "In transnational households one parent, both parents or adult children may be producing income abroad while other family members carry out the functions of reproduction, socialization, and consumption in the country of origin" (Zontini, 2007).

Issues to Ponder

1. Which is better for a young child?
   (A) To have a parent exit the labor force in order to provide direct care
   (B) To receive high-quality care in a center staffed by trained care providers

   In determining your conclusion, consider concerns such as socialization, physical health, engagement with peers, and physical safety. What situation would you prefer for you and your own child? How likely is it that you will be able to match your employment to your ideal childcare arrangement?

2. If the United States were to move toward paid family leave, how long should that leave be? Should incentives that encourage *both* mothers and fathers to take some time out of their jobs in order to provide care and bond with their children be included in this leave? What are some possible incentives?

3. Should the United States regulate work hours, such as a limit on the maximum work hours employees can be required to labor? If no, why not? If yes, what should that limit be? How would you design such a law?

4. There has been much talk about closing the borders in the United States to prevent illegal immigration, and this focuses on the supply side of the problem. An alternate is to focus on the demand side of the problem and to penalize employers who actively seek out these workers. Which is a more grievous crime, sneaking into a country to earn a living or sneaking around fair-labor standards to employ low-wage workers? What should happen to citizens in the United States who knowingly employ illegal immigrants to clean their houses, mow their lawns, watch their children, or care for their aging parents? Should they be imprisoned? Fined? Why or why not?

Mini Project

Exhibit 5.3 is a screen image of the public data directory provided by Google. Using this resource, examine the World Development Indicators and compare the United States to both a Western European society and a developing-economy society of your choice. Focus on issues such as child well-being, social development, health, life expectancy, and any other factors that might relate to effective integration of wage earning and caregiving. Especially focus on variables listed in "Labor and Social Protection." After performing your analysis, summarize the following:

- What were the most notable differences among nations?
- In what ways is the United States similar or dissimilar to developing nations?
- In what ways is the United States similar or dissimilar to Western European societies?
- Are countries converging or diverging over time?

Note: When you open the World Development Indicators page, use the lower left-hand panel to change "Compare by Region" to "Compare by Region–Country" using the drop-down menu. If an indicator is listed in italics then these data are not available for individual countries.

Exhibit 5.3   Google's Public Data Resources Offer Opportunities to Compare Indicators of Well-Being Across Societies

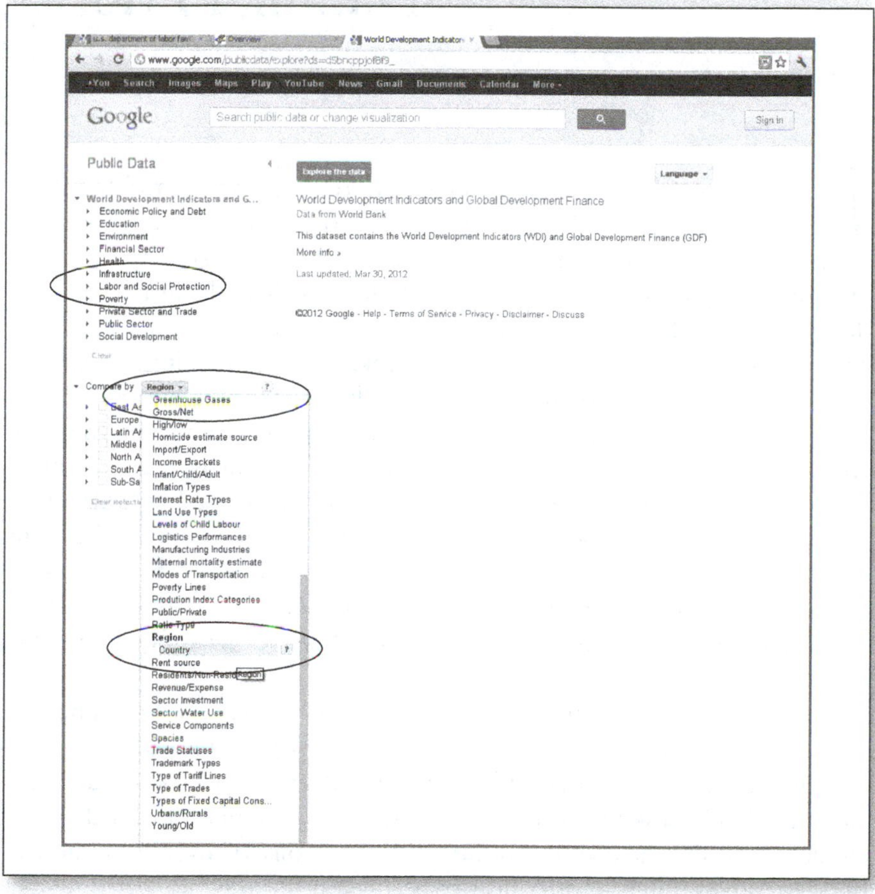

Source: www.google.com/publicdata/explore?ds=d5bncppjof8f9

6

Work-Family Interface as a National Priority

In 2011 I attended an international conference on work and family in Tampere, Finland. As has been the case at other conferences I traveled to, I found it interesting not only to learn of how workers and families are treated by other societies, but also the words and phrases used to describe these differences. For example, an Australian described her country as *only* entitling workers to 4 weeks of paid vacation. And while my colleagues and I try to position work-family concerns as agenda items in the United States, elsewhere nations are actively wrestling with work-family policies, trying to maximize their returns. For example, while the topic of paid family leave is scarcely mentioned by politicians in the United States, elsewhere policy makers are questioning the right amount of paid family leave to be specifically directed to fathers (1 month? 2 months? 3 months?) and testing whether these should be implemented *in addition to* the full year of leave (or more) available to mothers.

On the final evening, after the close of the conference, I sat down and had a beer at a pub. As the tables filled, an older Finnish man asked if he could sit with me. I learned that he had met Donald Rumsfeld when he was in his twenties, that he was a former civil servant, that he had never married or had children, and that he considered himself to be "conservative." On our second beer, I asked him to offer his perspective on the way his society works so as to verify a cultural difference between his world and mine. Below is a rough recounting of our conversation.

Me: So, let me ask you . . . you pay about half of your income in taxes, but in the U.S. we pay only about 25% in taxes.

Finn: Yes, that sounds right.

Me: And your taxes are going to things that you personally never benefit from.

Finn: Meaning?

Me: Well, for example, you didn't marry, and your taxes went to support women who took time out of the labor force. You pay for the health care of people who sometimes choose not to work, and much of your taxes are being used to provide for the needs of other people's children.

Finn: Yes, that is true.

Me: So because you don't benefit, wouldn't you prefer the American system?

Finn (eyes wide): No! I never complain about taxes, and I am a conservative. If those young people choose not to work, what is it to me? And I am fortunate, because I am healthy. But what would happen to me if I fell sick?

Me: So you wouldn't trade.

Finn: No way!

As this dialogue shows, if this man is typical (and he probably is), Finns would not want the American system. Conversely, many Americans would not want to trade either. But if we were to attempt to move the needle in a direction that would make the American system operate more like the Nordic systems, how would we do that? And what should we expect in response to efforts exerted? Key to this effort would be mobilizing government leaders to create legislation that facilitates work and family functioning. In suggesting six major government initiatives, the intent is not so much to lay out specific policies but rather to identify, in a broad sense, the avenues through which governments can reshape the contexts in which work-family relationships play out. Some of these initiatives are focused on the family sphere, some focus on the work sphere, and some are directly "work-family." But all share the prospect that the capacity to provide care and engage in secure, meaningful employment can be improved by placing work-family concerns on the national agenda. None of the suggestions are especially radical, but likely they would encounter resistance. So in addition to outlining what can potentially be done, identified are some of the reasons why these suggestions have not happened already.

Launching the Work-Family Field and the National Workplace Flexibility Initiative

Kathleen Christensen

In 1994 I founded and until 2011 directed the Alfred P. Sloan Foundation's Workplace, Workforce & Working Families program, having previously researched contingent staffing and flexible scheduling as a professor of psychology. Through strategic grant making and the contributions of dedicated grantees, this innovative program defined and legitimated the field of work-family research and translated the results to journalists, policymakers, and business leaders.

We funded more than 300 grants, totaling over $130 million; the first and by far largest commitment of resources dedicated to understanding what was happening to the American working family. These grants established the work-family field—including the Sloan Work and Family Research Network—resulting in 1,000 peer-reviewed articles, 100 books, and nearly 300 PhDs and postdoctoral fellows from diverse fields, including sociology, psychology, economics, anthropology, linguistics, education, labor relations, and management studies.

This interdisciplinary research documented that Americans were experiencing a severe time famine, often finding it difficult to meet the demands of both paid work and caregiving. Many parents felt torn between being a good worker and a good parent. It became clear to me that this was due to a structural mismatch between the rigid way work was structured in time and place and the needs of workers, who indicated they needed more control over when, where, and how they worked.

As a result, in 2003, we launched the National Workplace Flexibility Initiative, with the dual goals of making workplace flexibility a compelling national issue and the standard of the American workplace. The initiative adopted two funding strategies—increasing voluntary employer adoption of workplace flexibility and creating a new policy dialogue in Washington, D.C.—around flexibility. Among the many results of the initiative was the 2010 White House Forum on Workplace Flexibility convened by President Barack Obama and First Lady Michelle Obama.

Kathleen Christensen is a program director at the Alfred P. Sloan Foundation. Her writings are bookended by *Workplace Flexibility: Realigning 20th Century Jobs for a 21st Century Workforce* (Cornell University Press, 2010) and *Women and Home-Based Work: The Unspoken Contract* (Henry Holt, 1988).

What Governments Can Do

Whether by action or inaction, governments set terms of engagement that shape the work-family interface. But the extent of the government's role in directing social relations is a hotly debated issue in the United States. On one side are conservatives who argue against a "nanny state" and express concern over politicians setting standards that do not reflect mainstream values or interests. Their perspective cautions against relying on a set of socially removed legislators, who might craft policies that constrain choice and liberty. And this perspective casts a critical eye on regulatory actions as potentially stifling innovation and the creative spirit that drives capitalism. For that reason, advocates of this position argue that workers and employers should be empowered to set their own terms on how, when, and how much work is to be performed, and the less government "gets in the way" the better. When it comes to the redistribution of resources, government should not place a substantially heavier burden on the rich in order to provide resources to other less advantaged groups. When translated to government's role in resolving work-family concerns, the conservative perspective suggests a laissez-faire arrangement, one in which government remains (for the most part) disengaged in concerns related to work and family.

In comparison to its counterparts in Western Europe and most other advanced economies, the United States has leaned much further in the direction of this conservative laissez-faire approach, emphasizing autonomous personal responsibility as the path to resolving work and family concerns. In contrast, Western European governments have a longer history of proactive engagement in the resolution of work-family tensions. Progressive liberals advocate for this stance, arguing that governments can sway social relations in positive ways. What can governments do to affect the work-family interface?

First, *governments can regulate the terms of employment*. For example, if a society expects that most everyone is to work, a reciprocal expectation could be that employers provide reasonable compensation—and government can set the base of what constitutes a fair day's pay for a fair day's work (Ellwood, 1987). Consider, for example, that the federal minimum wage standard in the United States in 2012 was $7.25 per hour, approximately 3 to 4 dollars less than a livable wage in most communities. Not only can governments influence wage rates, they also can impose workplace safety, work hour, and job security standards. They can limit overt forms of discrimination (such as those that operate on the basis of gender, age, or parental status), as well as structural forms of discrimination (such as failure to provide facilities that enable breastfeeding; Still & Williams, 2006). Consider, for example, that France's 35-hour work week regulations strongly discourage employers from expecting workers to labor longer hours, and in the United Kingdom workers have a "right to request" shorter work hour arrangements. Both of these practices stand in stark contrast to the United States, where there are no effective work hour regulations, other than mandatory time-and-a-half overtime pay for workers who are "nonexempt" from the Fair Labor Standards Act legislation. All of these types of actions on the work front would directly affect the family front. When translated to the resolution of work-family concerns, the enforcement of safe work conditions, reasonable schedules, and job protections can result in numerous benefits on the family side that will not necessarily undermine productivity (Fagnani & Letablier, 2004; Krugman, 2005). The question for any society is what those standards should be. In determining the answer, the interests of both families and employers need to be taken into account.

Second, *governments can establish entitlements and base supports.* In the United States examples of entitlements include unemployment insurance that provides temporary compensation to those who have lost jobs; welfare and low-income supports (such as heating subsidies) that help buffer the consequences of poverty; and public school systems that provide educational opportunities irrespective of parental attachment to the labor force. Because the United States has not created entitlements that provide sufficient universal care supports for the elderly or young children, or established a national paid family leave policy that makes leave both widely available and affordable, many families experience difficulties in holding down paid employment while simultaneously caring for children or aging parents. And in an economy where jobs are less secure, workers in the United States are especially vulnerable. Consider, for example, that in the United States the maximum unemployment compensation that most eligible workers can receive is 50% of their wages (up to a capped amount) for a maximum of 26 weeks. Displaced workers in Denmark can receive 90% of their previous salary for a maximum of 2 years. Note, however, that this generous amount of time was halved from the previous standard of 4 years, in part because it was identified that when individuals are out of work for extended lengths of time, they face greater challenges in ever successfully reentering the labor force (Alderman, 2010). These types of adjustments indicate that societies not only need to identify the array of entitlements that should be offered, but also the costs involved, the thresholds at which positive gains are produced and lost, and other nuts-and-bolts design elements of how those entitlements operate (Thevenon & Guthier, 2011).

Third, *governments can redistribute collective resources.* Consider, as examples, how Social Security in the United States operates by transferring funds generated by currently working individuals to others out of the labor force; how funds generated in urban centers have been used to support rural development; and how schools are supported by taxes irrespective of the taxpayer's parental status. All of these practices, well integrated into the American system, involve taking resources from people and communities and reapplying them elsewhere where need is greater.

As Exhibit 6.1 shows, entitlement programs can be expensive, and as a result, taxes are substantially higher in Europe than in the United States. However, it could also be argued that the costs to families are not actually higher in Europe than they are in the United States, as in some instances the true costs are lower (such as in health care). The question is whether costs are to be paid directly out of pocket or through the tax base.

Exhibit 6.1 Government Public Expenditure as Percentage of GDP: International Comparisons 2005

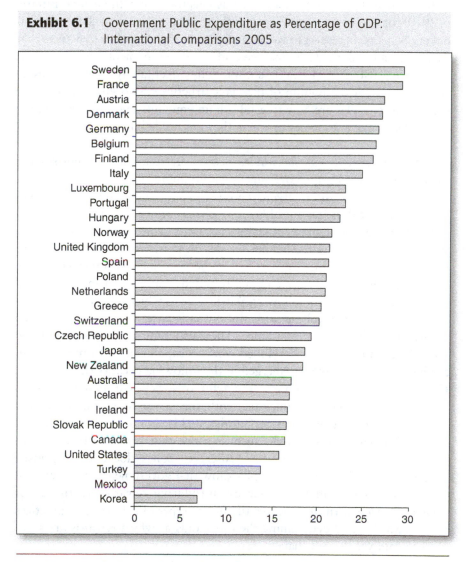

Source: Organisation for Economic Co-operation and Development (2010)

In the United States there has been a growing unwillingness to redistribute wealth downward through the class structure, and a previously more progressive tax system has been largely dismantled. Consider that in 2008 the richest fifth of households received half (50%) of the collective income earned, whereas the poorest fifth received only 3% (U.S. Census, 2011). In 1970, the marginal income tax rate on the highest earners was 71%, but by 2011, this had fallen to 35%. And through changes to provisions in the tax codes that exempt or reduce earnings on capital gains (investment earnings), the 1% top earners commonly paid taxes at rates much lower than members of the middle classes. Sometimes (such as was the case with General Electric in 2010) top-earning companies pay nothing in taxes and even claim substantial tax benefits. In respect to work-family concerns, the policy structures that enable substantial divides in income and wealth attainment, and those that prevent redistribution of wealth, substantially affect family well-being (especially of those at the bottom of the class structure). Two key questions for societies to consider are how to establish an equitable tax structure and the best ways to move resources to where they are needed most.

Fourth, *governments can incentivize behavior*. Numerous examples show the ways the United States government has attempted to influence the behavior of citizens through incentives. Those who stay in the labor force longer are rewarded with larger Social Security checks after retirement; those who put their money into retirement savings accounts avoid taxation on earnings; those who own homes receive tax breaks on mortgage interest; and those who improve their homes (such as by weatherproofing measures) receive tax write-offs. One of the most commonly noted examples of incentives and their impact is the GI Bill following World War II, which encouraged returning soldiers to enter college with tuition assistance and to assume home ownership with mortgage assistance. These economic resources helped fuel the baby boom, as well as developed workers capable of performing jobs in the high-tech economy that emerged in the following decades (Elder, 1986). Consider also that in response to the aging of societies, a number of other countries have been experimenting with incentives to encourage higher reproduction rates (Thevenon & Guthier, 2011). Numerous incentives are extended to employers as well, such as those that provide tax breaks to companies that move operations to "enterprise zones" located in depressed neighborhoods. All of these examples show that government can affect both sides of the work-family interface by introducing reward structures. For societies, key concerns include identifying the types of behaviors or practices to be rewarded and determining the thresholds at which rewards are sufficient to catalyze desired changes.

Fifth, *governments can establish international trade standards*. The global economy operates via complex supply chains that cross national boundaries. While governments can set standards for what occurs within their borders, they also can exercise leverage in shaping the terms of labor elsewhere. For example, the North American Free Trade Agreement includes environmental standards expected of all participating nations. The European Union agreements include a substantial attention to work conditions, setting standards for member nations on concerns such as use of child labor, maximum weekly work hours, and annual leave (vacation) rights. Governments also can elect to restrict trade with societies over concerns such as the infringement of human rights. When translated to work-family concerns, the use of international trade standards can be used as a carrot to positively affect the work conditions among trade partners (and to level the playing field among nations) and as a whip to penalize societies that undermine individual and family conditions with lax labor standards. Key for societies is how to determine these standards, a challenge because of the tremendous variation in cultural values and economic resources in the global economy. But as Tom Kochan (2005) argued, it is in the interests of American workers and their families to try to affect work standards elsewhere, in part to protect jobs and working conditions in the United States from a race to the bottom. Because other societies will accept work on any terms does not necessarily mean that the United States has to participate in trade with these nations. This is not to suggest isolationism, but it is possible to move other societies forward using the very same mechanisms that might compel a society to give up nuclear ambitions or end apartheid. By exerting pressures on other societies to establish quality work standards, these policies could also potentially affect family life quality.

Sixth, *governments can establish immigration standards*. In 2006, there were nearly 8 million undocumented workers laboring in the United States (Jaeger, 2006). While much of the discussion has been on how to keep illegal immigrants from crossing the U.S.–Mexican border, the prospect of deporting undocumented workers, and their family members, has proven to be a vexing problem for both Republican and Democratic parties. One of the current challenges is creating solutions to secure the interests of immigrant children, recognizing that some have lived nearly their whole lives in the United States.

Because immigration policy has an impact on industries that rely heavily on migrant labor—especially in agriculture—some politicians have suggested temporary "guest worker" visas as a solution. These guest workers would labor in a manner similar to workers in the Bracero program (used to supply Mexican labor during and following World War II). But so long as the spouses and children of guest workers are not considered in this equation, such a program would inevitably disrupt family lives, even if economic draws are sufficient motivators to bring in workers. If the focus remains restricted to the immigrant as the problem, rather than the economic needs and incentives to employ foreign-born workers, the problems associated with immigration will remain only partially managed, and family lives will be harmed as a consequence.

Government action can have a major impact on shaping the work-family interface by setting base standards for employment, providing entitlements and collective resources, redistributing wealth, incentivizing some behaviors and discouraging others, and setting international trade and immigration standards. None of these activities departs from past practice, as the United States (and other societies) has instituted many regulations with precisely these intents in mind. The question is where these standards should be moved in the future and the extent that work-family concerns influence the decision-making process.

Making the Case and Understanding Resistance

Establishing work-family harmonization as a national priority requires mobilizing collective support and understanding sources of resistance. The preceding chapters identified a number of reasons why the work-family interface should be part of a national agenda, but making this happen will not be easy because many stakeholders have interests in maintaining the status quo. Some will view taxes associated with entitlement initiatives as taking money out of their own pockets. Some will view revisions to wage, job security, or work hour standards as impinging on free enterprise. And political parties have very different visions of the role of government in the lives of people and workings of the economy.

In the current global economic crisis, some now look to struggling economies in Europe as having spent beyond their means on social entitlements (such as those that are critical to work-family harmonization). Japan, Italy, and other aging societies are facing related problems, as there will almost inevitably be too few workers to create revenue needed to support an older generation exiting from the workforce. (By 2050, 40% of the population of Japan is expected to be age 65 or older; Statistics Bureau of Japan, 2012.) There is great merit to the observation that revenue streams need to be sufficient to fund whatever society promises to provide and that these revenues need to be considered in respect to the near and distant futures. What is commonly lost in the discussion is that, in the case of the United States, there is a remarkable amount of potential revenue that could be directed to concerns such as childcare and elder care, but these resources are directed out of the public and into the private realm, or into other policy initiatives that have less bearing on the day-to-day lives of working families.

The argument that the United States "cannot afford" the standards of most other highly developed economies should not go unchallenged (Heymann & Earle, 2010). But if such a challenge is to be made, higher taxes, as well as a more progressive tax structure, will have to be part of the bargain. Many will not like this prospect. To counter resistance, compelling cases and rationale need to be formulated to enhance societal commitments to work and family concerns. Three basic arguments can be made—for social justice, economic productivity, and collective interests—and within each, work-family connections and consequences can be made paramount.

The argument for *social justice* focuses on inequality and inequity in the ways burdens, resources, and opportunities are allocated. If, for example, full-time women earners receive only 77 cents for every dollar full-time male earners receive, women do not share the same potential to establish economically viable families as do men. If job security rests on the expectation of full-time (or more) work commitments, without any career breaks, these expectations penalize workers who are scripted to perform various forms of care work—including parents and especially mothers. These types of observations can be directed at addressing economic resources available to working families and how the performance of care work is inequitably distributed and compensated. Or to take another example, if children who live in middle-class suburban communities can return to safe neighborhoods, but poor and minority children inhabiting urban and rural communities cannot, this can be used to legitimize attention to afterschool care concerns. In each case, attention is directed at the floor (what some members of society lack) and the disparity of their condition relative to the middle (what most members of society possess) and the ceiling (what is accessible to the most privileged members of society). Note, however, that social justice arguments are sometimes reframed as "class warfare," as redistribution of resources is a common objective, as is the introduction of various protections for those most disadvantaged.

The social justice argument should neither be overestimated nor underestimated in its potential impact on the trajectory of work-family initiatives. The civil rights movement, for example, rested primarily on this foundation. So did the passage of the Americans with Disabilities Act, which mandated reasonable accommodations for workers with disabilities and access to public buildings. Some have argued that similar strategies can be used to advance programs such as paid family leave (Feldblum & Appleberry, 2006). However, recognize that those who are most affected by work-family strains—especially the poor, children, women, and the frail elderly—tend to have weak voices in policy debates. For this reason, it should not be expected that the social justice argument will carry force on empathy alone. It will require increasing the representation of elected officials who understand the concerns of the disadvantaged and are willing to herald their interests. That only 17% of elected members of Congress in 2012 were women and very few members came from working-class backgrounds can explain why concerns such as access to affordable, quality day care are not part of the legislative agenda (Kunin, 2012).

The argument for workplace productivity was introduced in Chapter 4, which focuses on employer interests in being family responsive. To the extent that work-family supports can translate to a broader national *economic productivity*, this can be a means of establishing both the need for—and support of—a work-family agenda. Toward that end, government can play a role in promoting and rewarding organizations that push workplace standards forward or, conversely, withdraw discretionary supports for those that do not. This is an important component of the work-family agenda. However, so long as family-responsive employment practices remain exclusively voluntary, a full expansion of universally available rights and resources is unlikely to be achieved through the productivity rationale. While the focus on identifying potentially positive workplace outcomes can be a component of a national agenda, it cannot stand on its own without attention being drawn to issues of equity and interests that go beyond the concerns of corporations. Consider, for example, that the Family Medical Leave Act (FMLA), which provides opportunity for 12 weeks of unpaid leave, was resisted by employers and groups such as the Chamber of Commerce on the basis of anticipated costs to be incurred by private enterprise. Similar arguments are raised today regarding the right to paid time off for illness. One statistic helped propel passage of the FMLA: *not* having access to leave resulted in far more substantial costs to families than the costs anticipated to be incurred by employers (Hartmann, 2012). The point here is that it is important to bring employers on board in a national agenda, but these efforts cannot stand independent of a focus on social justice and collective interests. And it is equally important to recognize that national economic well-being is not equivalent to the sum of corporate profits.

The argument for *collective interests* focuses on the implications of inattention to concerns that fully or partially originate from work-family tensions and the ramifications not only for those directly involved, but also for the broader society. Consider, for example, how the creation of a competitive workforce is linked to the work-family interface or how the containment of health costs might be linked to harmonizing work and family connections. The United States has among the highest teen birth rates among comparable nations with advanced economies. It also has among the highest childhood obesity, substance abuse, and imprisonment rates. All of these concerns affect the greater good. To the extent that work-family factors are identified as contributing to broader societal problems, arguments can be made to adjust work-family configurations in response. Of course work-family tensions are not the only source of the problems just mentioned, but they are contributing factors. As economist Jared Bernstein (2006) argued, collective interests can be a fundamental basis for a variety of reforms that include and go beyond work-family concerns, but it will require moving the culture away from accepting a "you're on your own" mentality to a "we're in it together" commitment.

In all likelihood, "let's harmonize work-family" is not going to be an effective rally cry to move work-family concerns to center stage. And perhaps "women's interests," "children's interests," or the interests of any restricted specific set of stakeholders will not be a sufficient catalyst either. Instead, what may hold more promise is identifying concerns that cut across social groups to generate support from broad coalitions of diverse populations. For example, paid family leave entitlements may be resisted because they are perceived as restrictive (relevant just to women) and unaffordable. While neither perception is true, many people and veto groups may continue to act with this assumption in mind, and they will be well positioned to undermine prospects for reform. In contrast, rights to paid time off are far less restrictive and cut across gender lines. Support might be further boosted by showing how policy initiatives affect collective interests (such as the negative impact sick workers have on coworkers and clientele). When political leaders champion objectives related to the work-family interface, some bold policy initiatives may be successful. Less bold initiatives that increase capacities to provide care, work outside the home, and exit the labor force when family needs emerge might also be nudged along. The rationale that underpins the causes of social justice, economic productivity, and collective interests can lend weight and momentum to arguments made on behalf of a work-family agenda.

Conclusion

Experiences in the workplace and home can provide some of the highest highs and lowest lows. Involvement in both spheres not only engages most waking time, it requires intense physical and psychological engagement. This book outlines the friction that can result from competing institutional expectations and consequences for workers, their families, their employers, and their societies. But also it illustrates that work-family arrangements are not only problems to solve, but also elements of life to appreciate. Even with all of the challenges from the complex commitments in the home and workplace, for most people, their lives are richer as a result.

What will be done to reconcile the chafing aspects of work and family is a matter of choice. There may be some natural evolution, such that lagging parts of either the culture or the structure in which it operates catch up to one another. Young men want to be more engaged in care work than their fathers and far more so than their grandfathers were. These desires may result in meaningful change as generational replacement occurs, but they will confront structural arrangements that will need to be adjusted accordingly. Old boundaries that separated women from opportunities in the workplace continue to be dismantled, and yet glass ceilings and sticky floors will continue to have a differential impact on men's and women's careers and in turn shape their commitments to their families. Employers are experimenting with programs that expand opportunities to engage in flexible work, demonstrating that new arrangements can satisfy a dual agenda. However, other employers have yet to come on board, and some are unlikely to do so. Although most work-family scholars believe that efforts of the U.S. government to address concerns have been inadequate, the government has been increasingly engaged in regulating work and family concerns, such as with entitlements for (alas, still unpaid) family leave and required employee access to facilities that enable breastfeeding in the workplace. These types of observations lead one to be optimistic about the future direction of work-family policy, but not to have a blind faith that progress will be inevitable.

The problems from work-family incompatibility present serious concerns not only for working families, but also their employers and societies. So long as children, spouses, neighbors, or other kin go without care as a result of work demands, the objective of harmonized lives will be unrealized. So long as work fails to provide adequate financial resources, or undermines physical or psychological well-being, negative spillover will result. One would hope that personal family and career goals can be further enhanced by considering the interplay of work and home demands. In resolving these issues, equity needs to be paramount so that access to resources is available to those with the greatest needs. The status quo in the United States demands far too much from families and far too little from their employers and government. The more this society recognizes that family and work concerns are intertwined, the easier it will be to make a compelling case for the bold changes needed.

Useful Concepts

Living wage. "The living wage level is usually the wage a full-time worker would need to earn to support a family above the federal poverty line, ranging from 100% to 130% of the poverty measurement" (Economic Policy Institute, 2002).

Minimum wage. "A minimum rate of pay that firms are legally obliged to pay their workers. Most industrial countries have a minimum wage, although certain sorts of workers are often exempted, such as young people or part-timers" (Economist, 2012).

Statutory entitlement. A resource that people are entitled to receive as stipulated by law. Common examples are unemployment compensation and Social Security Insurance (Gornick & Meyers, 2003).

Issues to Ponder

1. Suppose you had a choice, to live in a society where half your income is taxed but where every citizen has access to health care, childcare, and family leave, or in a society where only about one-fifth of your income is taxed but where many lack access to health care, childcare, or family leave options. Which would you choose?

2. Is it the role of government to identify the best means of maximizing the resources available to everyone? And is it within that role to reallocate wealth from those who are most successful to those who are most needy? Or alternately, is the role of government simply to protect its citizens and provide only for the basic needs to keep society operating?

Mini Projects

1. Using an Internet search tool such as Google, research the entitlements and protections available in any society of your choosing. For example, search "unemployment compensation" and "Italy." Try to locate the national policies or standards for resources relevant to work and family functioning. Some phrases you might include in your search are the following:
   - Unemployment compensation
   - Job protections
   - Childcare

- o Elder care
- o Family Leave
- o Taxes
- o Work hour limits
- o Health care coverage
- o Health care expense
- o Quality of life
- o Happiness
- o Vacation entitlements
- o Paid leave

2. Try to construct a "Family Bill of Rights," a statement outlining certain things all families in the United States should have access to. After composing your Family Bill of Rights, look at the one constructed by Take Care Net and consider whether you would want to add any items identified in this resource (www.takecarenet.org/WorkFamilyBOR.aspx).

Then consider the extent to which whatever you identified is universally accessible. If it is not, why is it not available?

3. Try to construct a "Workers' Bill of Rights," a statement outlining certain things all employees in the United States should have access to. Then consider the extent to which whatever you identified is universally accessible. If it is not, why is it not available?

4. Consider any work-family policy of your choice (e.g., affordable childcare, paid family leave, increased minimum wage standards) and try to articulate a social justice, business, and collective interest case for that argument. See if you can find any relevant supporting data to support your argument (e.g., unequal access or risk to specific groups, potential cost savings to employers or societies). Of the three arguments to be made, which rationale provided the most compelling case for your stance?

Further Exploration

One of the strengths of work-family scholarship is that it draws upon the insights of multiple disciplines, including sociology, psychology, business, economics, history, gender/family studies, demography, anthropology, and law. However, because many library search tools are discipline specific, conventional means of locating work-family research can leave many stones unturned.

For those interested in developing expertise in work and family concerns, I recommend two handbooks that consider in detail issues of disciplinary focus, research design, and practice.

- Pitt-Catsouphes, Marcie, Ellen Kossek, and Stephen Sweet. 2006. *The Work and Family Handbook: Multi-Disciplinary Perspectives, Methods and Approaches*. Mahwah, NJ: Lawrence Erlbaum.
- Korabik, Karen, Donna Lero and Denise Whitehead. 2008. *Handbook of Work-Family Integration: Research, Theory and Best Practices*. New York: Academic Press.

In addition to these books, those interested in specific concerns related to work and family can benefit by accessing the resources developed by the Work and Family Researchers Network (formerly the Sloan Work and Family Research Network). WFRN provides a wealth of resources (http://workfamily .sas.upenn.edu), including the *Work and Family Encyclopedia* with an in-depth analysis of key concerns central to work-family inquiry, a glossary of relevant concepts that far surpasses the limited number of definitions provided in this book, and identification of key work-family scholars. The WFRN provides many teaching-related resources, such as course syllabi and class activities for those interested in teaching work-family concepts, and it offers presentations of business-related solutions to work-family concerns, including descriptions of employers who have reconfigured their work designs. The WFRN also supplies current information on work-family conferences, events, and recent news, as well as identifies scholarly research.

The Work and Family Researchers Network

Judi C. Casey

For 5 years, I was the principle investigator and director of the Sloan Work and Family Research Network, the premier online destination for work and family information for academics, corporate practitioners, and public policy makers. After 14 years of funding from the Alfred P. Sloan Foundation, the project received a final grant to create a new organization that continues the efforts of the Network and the legacy established by the Sloan Foundation.

The new Work and Family Researchers Network (WFRN) is an international membership organization of interdisciplinary work and family researchers. While membership is geared toward the global community of work and family academics and scholars—including faculty, staff, students, teachers, and researchers—policy makers, practitioners, journalists, and interested others are encouraged to get involved. The WFRN was formed in response to the need for a membership association of interdisciplinary work and family scholars. Unique among professional societies, the WFRN facilitates virtual and face-to-face interaction among work and family researchers from a broad range of fields and engages the next generation of work and family scholars. As a global hub, we provide opportunities for information sharing and networking via our website, which includes a News Feed and the only open-access work and family subject matter repository, the Work and Family Commons.

One of the major changes from the Sloan Network to the WFRN is the transformation from a staff-driven enterprise to a member-driven one. Members will take leadership roles in running all facets of the organization and in providing content of interest to the interdisciplinary work and family research community. For the WFRN to succeed, we need the global community interested in work and family to get involved. Their support will help to advance, promote, and preserve interdisciplinary work and family scholarship to move the field forward.

Please visit our website at https://workfamily.sas.upenn.edu.

References

Alderman, Liz. 2010. "Denmark Starts to Trim Its Admired Safety Net." *New York Times,* August 16, B1. www.nytimes.com/2010/08/17/business/global/17denmark .html?pagewanted=all.

Allen, Tammy. 2001. "Family-Supportive Work Environments: The Role of Organizational Perceptions." *Journal of Vocational Behavior* 58:414–35.

Altucher, Kristine and Lindy B. Williams. 2003. "Family Clocks: Timing Parenthood." Pp. 49–59 in *It's About Time: Career Strains, Strategies, and Successes,* edited by P. Moen. Ithaca, NY: Cornell University Press.

Arnett, Jeffrey. 2004. *Emerging Adulthood: The Winding Road from the Late Teens Through the Twenties.* New York: Oxford University Press.

———. 2007. "Afterword: Aging out of care: Toward realizing the possibilities of emerging adulthood." *New Directions for Youth Development* 113: 151–62.

Auslander, Mark. 2002. "Rituals of the Workplace." *Work and Famly Research Network Encyclopedia.* http://workfamily.sas.upenn.edu/wfrn-repo/object/ kz4cq542lr76qf4w.

Bacigalupe, Gonzalo. 2010. "Is Balancing Work and Family a Sustainable Metaphor?" *Journal of Feminist Family Therapy* 13:5–20.

Bailyn, Lotte, Ann Bookman, Mona Harrington, and Thomas Kochan. 2006. "Work-Family Interventions and Experiments: Workplaces, Communities, and Society." Pp. 651–64 in *The Work and Family Handbook: Multidisciplinary Perspectives, Methods, and Approaches,* edited by M. Pitt-Catsouphes, E. E. Kossek, and S. Sweet. Mahwah, NJ: Lawrence Erlbaum.

Bailyn, Lotte, Robin Collins, and Yang Song. 2007. "Self-Scheduling for Hospital Nurses: An Attempt and Its Difficulties." *Journal of Nursing Management* 15:72–77.

Ball, Howard. 2002. *The Supreme Court in the Intimate Lives of Americans: Birth, Sex, Marriage, Childrearing, and Death.* New York: New York University Press.

Barboza, David. 2010a. "After Suicides, Scrutiny of China's Grim Factories." *New York Times,* June 6. www.nytimes.com/2010/06/07/business/global/07suicide .html?pagewanted=all&_r=0.

———. 2010b. "A Night at the Electronics Factory." *New York Times,* June 19. www .nytimes.com/2010/06/20/weekinreview/20barboza.html.

Barnett, Rosalind Chait and Karen C. Gareis. 2000. "Reduced-Hours Employment: The Relationship between Difficulty of Trade-Offs and Quality of Life." *Work and Occupations* 27:168–87.

Barnett, Rosalind Chait, Karen Gareis, Judith Gordon, and Robert Brennan. 2009. "Usable Flexibility, Employee's Concerns About Elders, Gender, and Job Withdrawal." *The Psychologist-Manager Journal* 12:50–71.

Barnett, Rosalind Chait, Sandee Shulkin, Karen Gareis, and Kimberly Kopko. 2008. "After-School Care and Work-Life Issues." *Sloan Work and Family Encyclopedia.* http://workfamily.sas.upenn.edu/wfrn-repo/object/1ly6y4r8t0ah0l36.

Becker, Penny Edgell and Phyllis Moen. 1999. "Scaling Back: Dual-Earner Couples' Work-Family Strategies." *Journal of Marriage and the Family* 61:995–1007.

Beggren, Heidi. 2010. "Separate Spheres: Institutionalizing an Ideology." *Sloan Work and Family Encyclopedia.* http://workfamily.sas.upenn.edu/wfrn-repo/object/u71875ti9x9dy6k5.

Bernstein, Jared. 2006. *All Together Now: Common Sense for a Fair Economy.* San Francisco: Berrett-Koehler.

Bookman, Ann. 2004. *Starting in Our Own Backyards: How Working Families Can Build Community and Survive the New Economy.* New York: Routledge.

Bookman, Ann and Delia Kimbrel. 2011. "Families and Elder Care in the Twenty-First Century." *Future of Children* 21:117–40.

Booth, Alan and Ann C. Crouter. 2000. *Does it Take a Village? Community Effects on Children, Adolescents, and Families.* Mahwah, NJ: Lawrence Erlbaum.

Boris, Eileen and Carolyn Lewis. 2006. "Caregiving and Wage-Earning: A Historical Perspective on Work and Family." Pp. 73–98 in *The Work and Family Handbook: Multidisciplinary Perspectives, Methods and Approaches*, edited by M. Pitt-Catsouphes, E. E. Kossek, and S. Sweet. Mahwah, NJ: Lawrence Erlbaum.

Boyar, Scott, Carl Maertz, and Allison Pearson. 2005. "The Effects of Work-Family Conflict and Family-Work Conflict on Nonattendance Behaviors." *Journal of Business Research* 58:919–25.

Broder, John. 2006. "Immigrants and the Economics of Hard Work." *New York Times,* April 2, WK 3.

Buettner, Dan. 2008. *Blue Zones: Lessons for Living Longer from the People Who've Lived the Longest.* New York: National Geographic Press.

Caligiuri, Paula and Mila Lazarova. 2005. "Work-Life Balance and the Effective Management of Global Assignees." Pp. 121–46 in *Work and Family: An International Research Perspective*, edited by S. Poelmans. Mahwah, NJ: Lawrence Erlbaum.

Camayd-Freixas, Erik. 2008. "Interpreting After the Largest ICE Raid in US History: A Personal Account." *New American Media.* http://graphics8.nytimes.com/images/2008/07/14/opinion/14ed-camayd.pdf.

Cappelli, Peter. 2008. *Talent on Demand: Managing Talent in an Age of Uncertainty.* Cambridge, MA: Harvard Business School Press.

Celello, Kristin. 2009. *Making Marriage Work: A History of Marriage and Divorce in the Twentieth-Century United States.* Chapel Hill: University of North Carolina Press.

Christensen, Kathleen and Ralph Gomory. 1999. "Three Jobs, Two People." *Washington Post,* June 2, A21.

Chronicle of Higher Education. 2010. "Chronicle of Higher Education Almanac." http://chronicle.com/section/Almanac-of-Higher-Education/463.

College Board. 2011. *Trends in College Pricing 2011.* http://trends.collegeboard.org/college_pricing.

Connelly, Rachel, Deborah Degraff, and Rachel Willis. 2002. "If You Build It They Will Come: Parental Use of On-Site Child Care Centers." *Population Research and Policy Review* 21:241–73.

Coontz, Stephanie. 2000. *The Way We Never Were: American Families and the Nostalgia Trap.* New York: Basic Books.

Coser, Lewis. 1974. *Greedy Institutions: Patterns of Undivided Commitment.* New York: Free Press.

Crittenden, Ann. 2001. *The Price of Motherhood.* New York: Henry Holt.

Crosnoe, Robert and Glenn Elder. 2002. "Successful Adaptation in the Later Years: A Life Course Approach to Aging." *Social Psychology Quarterly* 65:309–28.

Crouter, Ann and Alan Booth. 2004. *Work-Family Challenges for Low-Income Parents and Their Children.* Mahwah, NJ: Lawrence Erlbaum.

Darrah, Charles. 2006. "Ethnography and Working Families." Pp. 367–86 in *The Work and Family Handbook: Multidisciplinary Perspectives, Methods and Approaches,* edited by M. Pitt-Catsouphes, E. E. Kossek, and S. Sweet. Mahwah, NJ: Lawrence Erlbaum.

Davis, Amy and Arne Kalleberg. 2006. "Family-Friendly Organizations? Work and Family Programs in the 1990s." *Work and Occupations* 33:191–223.

Davis, Shannon and Theodore Greenstein. 2009. "Gender Ideology: Components, Predictors, and Consequences." *Annual Review of Sociology* 35:87–105.

Desrochers, Stephan. 2003. "Boundary/Border Theory and Work-Family Integration." *Sloan Work and Family Encyclopedia.* http://workfamily.sas.upenn.edu/wfrn-repo/object/6uq9g6l9xc25a61t.

Deutsch, Francine. 1999. *Halving It All: How Equally Shared Parenting Works.* Cambridge, MA: Harvard University Press.

DiMaggio, Paul and Walter Powell. 1983. "The Iron Cage Revisited: Institutional Isomorphism and Collective Rationality in Organizational Fields." *American Sociological Review* 48:147–60.

Drago, Robert and Doug Hyatt. 2003. "Symposium: The Effect of Work-Family Policies on Employees and Employers." *Industrial Relations* 42:139–45.

Duhigg, Charles and David Barboza. 2012. "THE IECONOMY: In China, the Human Costs Are Built into an iPad." *New York Times,* January 25. www.nytimes.com/2012/01/26/business/ieconomy-apples-ipad-and-the-human-costs-for-workers-in-china.html?pagewanted=all.

Eaton, Susan. 2003. "If You Can Use Them: Flexibility Policies, Organizational Commitment, and Perceived Performance." *Industrial Relations* 42:145–67.

Economic Policy Institute. 2002. "EPI Issue Guide: Living Wage." www.liunabuildsamerica.org/files/reports/LivingWageIssueGuide.pdf.

Economist. 2012. "Economics A–Z." www.economist.com/economics-a-to-z.

Elder, Glen. 1986. "Military Times and Turning Points in Men's Lives." *Developmental Pathology* 22:233–45.

Ellwood, David. 1987. *Divide and Conquer: Responsible Security for America's Poor.* New York: Ford Foundation.

Evans, Clifford and Amanda Diekman. 2009. "On Motivated Role Selection: Gender Beliefs, Distant Goals, and Career Interest." *Psychology of Women Quarterly* 33:235–49.

Fagnani, Jeanne and Marie-Therese Letablier. 2004. "Work and Family Life Balance: The Impact of the 35 Hour Laws in France." *Work, Employment and Society* 18:551–72.

Feldblum, Chai Rachel and Robin Appleberry. 2006. "Legislatures, Agencies, Courts, and Advocates: How Laws Are Made, Interpreted, and Modified." Pp. 627–51 in *The Work and Family Handbook: Multi-Disciplinary Perspectives, Methods and Approaches*, edited by M. Pitt-Catsouphes, E. E. Kossek, and S. Sweet. Mahwah, NJ: Lawrence Erlbaum.

Franco, Jaime, Laura Sabattini, and Faye Crosby. 2004. "Anticipating Work and Family: Exploring the Associations Among Gender-Related Ideologies, Values, and Behaviors in Latino and White Families in the United States." *Journal of Social Issues* 60:755–66.

Friedan, Betty. 1963. *The Feminine Mystique.* New York: Norton.

Friedman, Dana E. 2001. "Caring for Infants and Toddlers." *The Future of Children* 11:62–77.

Galinsky, Ellen. 1999. *Ask the Children: What America's Children Really Think About Working Parents.* New York: William Morrow.

Galinsky, Ellen and James T. Bond. 1998. *The National Study of the Changing Work Force.* New York: Families and Work Institute.

Garey, Anita Ilta. 1999. *Weaving Work and Motherhood.* Philadelphia: Temple University Press.

Gerson, Kathleen. 2001. "Children of the Gender Revolution: Some Theoretical Questions and Findings from the Field." Pp. 446–61 in *Restructuring Work and the Life Course*, edited by V. W. Marshall, W. R. Heinz, H. Krueger, and A. Verma. Toronto: University of Toronto Press.

Gerstel, Naomi. 2011. "Rethinking Families and Community: The Color, Class and Centrality of Extended Kin Ties." *Sociological Forum* 26:1–20.

Gerstel, Naomi and Natalia Sarkesian. 2006. "Marriage: The Good, The Bad, and the Greedy." *Contexts* 5:16–22.

Gitelson, Idy and Dana McDermott. 2006. "Parents and Their Young Adult Children: Transitions to Adulthood." *Child Welfare* 85:853–66.

Golden, Lonnie. 1998. *Family Friend or Foe? Working Time, Flexibility, and the Fair Labor Standards Act.* Washington, D.C.: Economic Policy Institute.

———. 2001a. "Flexible Work Schedules: What Are We Trading to Get Them?" *Monthly Labor Review*, March:50–66.

———. 2001b. "Flexible Work Schedules: Which Workers Get Them?" *American Behavioral Scientist* 44:1157–78.

———. 2005. "Overemployment in the US: Which Workers Face Downward Constrained Hours." Pp. 209–34 in *Decent Working Time: New Trends, New Issues*, edited by Y. Boulin, J. Lallement, J. Messenger, and F. Michon. New York: International Labor Organization.

———. 2009. "Flexible Daily Work Schedules in the U.S. Jobs: Formal Introductions Needed?" *Industrial Relations* 48:27–54.

Goldscheider, F. and C. Goldscheider. 1999. *The Changing Transition to Adulthood: Leaving and Returning Home*. Thousand Oaks, CA: Sage.

Goldscheider, Frances, Arland Thornton, and Li-Shou Yang. 2001. "Helping Out the Kids: Expectations about Parental Support in Young Adulthood." *Journal of Marriage and Family* 63:727–40.

Gornick, Janet and Marcia Meyers. 2003. *Families that Work: Policies for Reconciling Parenthood and Employment*. New York: Russell Sage Foundation.

Grall, Timothy. 2009. "Custodial Mothers and Fathers and Their Child Support: 2007." Current Population Reports P60-237, edited by U.S. C. Bureau. Washington, D.C.

Gratton, Brian and Jon Moen. 2004. "Immigration, Culture, and Child Labor in the United States, 1880–1920." *Journal of Interdisciplinary History* 34:355–91.

———. 2007. "Child Labor: A Historical Perspective." *Work-Family Encyclopedia* http://wfnetwork.bc.edu/encyclopedia_entry.php?id=6335&area=academics.

Greenhaus, Jeffrey H. and Nicholas J. Beutell. 1985. "Sources of Conflict between Work and Family Roles." *Academy of Management Review* 10:76–88.

Greenhaus, Jeffrey H. and Romila Singh. 2003. "Work-Family Linkages." *Sloan Work and Family Encyclopedia*. http://workfamily.sas.upenn.edu/wfrn-repo/object/is5jc110dr1wn4q9.

Greenhouse, Steven. 2011. "Wage Protection for Home Care Workers." *New York Times*, October 15, B2. www.nytimes.com/2011/12/16/business/wage-protection-planned-for-home-care-workers.html.

Greenstein, Theodore. 1996. "Gender Ideology and Perceptions of the Fairness of the Division of Household Labor: Effects on Marital Quality." *Social Forces* 74:1029–42.

Grzywacz, Joseph and Adam Butler. 2008. "Schedule Flexibility and Stress: Linking Formal Flexible Arrangements and Perceived Flexibility to Employee Health." *Community, Work & Family* 11:199–214.

Grzywacz, Joseph and Jenna Tucker. 2008. "Work-Family Experiences and Physical Health: A Summary and Critical Review." *Work and Family Encyclopedia* http://wfnetwork.bc.edu/encyclopedia_entry.php?id=6410&area=All.

Haas, Linda and Tine Rostgaard. 2011. "Fathers' Rights to Paid Parental Leave in the Nordic Countries: Consequences for the Gendered Division of Leave." *Community, Work & Family* 14:179–97.

Hacker, Jacob. 2006. *The Great Risk Shift: The Assault on American Jobs, Families, Health Care and Retirement and How You Can Fight Back*. New York: Oxford University Press.

Hakim, Catherine. 2001. *Work-Lifestyle Choices in the Twenty-First Century*. New York: Oxford.

———. 2002. "Lifestyle Preferences as Determinants of Women's Differentiated Labor Market Careers." *Work and Occupations* 29:428–59.

Hareven, Tamara. 1982. *Family Time and Industrial Time: The Relationship Between the Family and Work in a New England Industrial Community*. New York: Cambridge University Press.

Hareven, Tamara and Randolph Langenbach. 1978. *Amoskeag*. New York: Pantheon Books.

Hartmann, Heidi. 2012. "Work and Family in the Context of a Feminist Policy Agenda." Work and Family Researchers Network Conference Presentation, June 16. New York.

Hattery, Angela. 2001. "Tag-Team Parenting: Costs and Benefits of Utilizing Nonoverlapping Shift Work in Families with Young Children." *Families in Society* 82:410–27.

Hegewisch, Ariane and Janet Gornick. 2008. "Statutory Routes to Workplace Flexibility in Cross-National Perspective." Institute for Women's Policy Research, Washington, D.C.

Heymann, Jody. 2000. *The Widening Gap: Why America's Working Families Are in Jeopardy and What Can Be Done About It*. New York: Perseus.

Heymann, Jody and Alison Earle. 2010. *Raising the Global Floor: Dismantling the Myth that We Can't Afford Good Working Conditions for Everyone*. Stanford, CA: Stanford University Press.

Heymann, Jody, Alison Earle, and Amresh Hanchate. 2004. "Bringing a Global Perspective to Community, Work, and Family." *Community, Work & Family* 7:247–71.

Hochschild, Arlie Russell. 1997. *The Time Bind: When Work Becomes Home and Home Becomes Work*. New York: Metropolitan Books.

———. 1999. "The Nanny Chain." *American Prospect* 11:32–36.

———. 2000. "Global Care Chains and Emotional Surplus Value." Pp. 130–46 in *Global Capitalism*, edited by W. Hutton and A. Giddens. New York: The New Press.

Hogan, Dennis P. 1980. "The Transition to Adulthood as a Career Contingency." *American Sociological Review* 45:261–76.

Hogan, Dennis P. and Nan Marie Astone. 1986. "The Transition to Adulthood." *Annual Review of Sociology* 12:109–30.

Holmes, Mary. 2009. "Commuter Couples and Distance Relationships: Living Apart Together." *Sloan Work and Family Encyclopedia*. http://workfamily.sas.upenn.edu/wfrn-repo/object/kb4p09ba3ur8c8di.

Hostetler, Andrew, Stephen Sweet, and Phyllis Moen. 2007. "Gendered Career Paths: A Life Course Perspective on the Return to School." *Sex Roles* 56:85–103.

Hutchens, Robert and Karen Grace-Martin. 2006. "Employer Willingness to Permit Phased Retirement: Why Are Some More Willing Than Others?" *Industrial and Labor Relations Review* 59:525–46.

Isaksen, Lise Widding, Sambaasivan Uma Devi, and Arlie Russell Hochschild. 2008. "Global Care Crisis: A Problem of Capital, Care Chain, or Commons." *American Behavioral Scientist* 52:405–25.

Jacoby, Sanford. 1991. *Masters to Managers.* New York: Columbia University Press.

Jaeger, David. 2006. "Replacing the Undocumented Work Force." Center for American Progress. www.americanprogress.org/issues/immigration/news/2006/04/04/1905/replacing-the-undocumented-work-force.

Kalleberg, Arne. 2009. "Precarious Work, Insecure Workers: Employment Relations in Transition." *American Sociological Review* 74:1–22.

Kan, Man Yee. 2007. "Work Orientation and Wives' Employment Careers: An Evaluation of Hakim's Preference Theory." *Work and Occupations* 34:430–62.

Kawamura, Sayaka and Susan Brown. 2010. "Mattering and Wives' Perceived Fairness of the Division of Household Labor." *Social Science Research* 39:976–86.

Kelliher, Clare and Deirdre Anderson. 2010. "Doing More with Less? Flexible Working Practices and the Intensification of Work." *Human Relations* 63:83–106.

Kelly, Erin. 2003. "The Strange History of Employer-Sponsored Child Care: Interested Actors, Uncertainty, and the Transformation of Law in Organizational Fields." *American Journal of Sociology* 109:606–49.

Kelly, Erin and Alexandra Kalev. 2006. "Managing Flexible Work Arrangements in US Organizations: Formalized Discretion or 'Right to Ask.'" *Socio-Economic Review* 4:379–416.

Kelly, Erin, Ellen Ernst Kossek, Leslie Hammer, Mary Durham, Jeremy Bray, Kelly Chermack, et al. 2008. "Getting There from Here: Research on the Effects of Work-Family Initiatives on Work-Family Conflict and Business Outcomes." Pp. 305–49 in *The Academy of Management Annals (Volume 2)*, edited by J. Walsh and A. Brief.

Kelly, Erin, Phyllis Moen, and Eric Tranby. 2011. "Changing Workplaces to Reduce Work-Family Conflict: Schedule Control in a White-Collar Organization." *American Sociological Review* 76:265–90.

Kochan, Thomas. 2005. *Restoring the American Dream: A Working Families' Agenda for America.* Cambridge, MA: MIT Press.

Kopelman, Richard, David Prottas, Cynthia Thompson, and Eileen White Jahn. 2006. "A Multilevel Examination of Work-Life Practices: Is More Always Better?" *Journal of Management Issues* 18:232–53.

Kossek, Ellen Ernst and Alyssa Fried. 2006. "The Business Case: Managerial Perspectives on Work and Family." Pp. 611–26 in *The Work and Family Handbook: Multidisciplinary Perspectives, Methods, and Approaches*, edited by M. Pitt-Catsouphes, E. E. Kossek, and S. Sweet. Mahwah, NJ: Lawrence Erlbaum.

Kossek, Ellen Ernst and Brenda Lautsch. 2012. "Work-Family Boundary Management Styles in Organizations: A Cross-Level Model." *Organizational Psychology Review* 2:152–71.

Kossek, Ellen Ernst, Brenda Lautsch, and Susan Eaton. 2004. "Flexibility Enactment Theory: Flexibility Type, Control, and Boundary Management for Work and Family Effectiveness." Pp. 233–50 in *Work and Life Integration: Organizational, Cultural and* Individual *Perspectives*, edited by E. E. Kossek and S. Lambert. Mahwah, NJ: Lawrence Erlbaum.

Kossek, Ellen Ernst and Cynthia Ozeki. 1999. "Bridging the Work-Family Policy and Productivity Gap." *Community, Work & Family* 2:7–32.

Kotsadam, Andreas and Henning Finseraas. 2011. "The State Intervenes in the Battle of the Sexes: Causal Effects of Paternity Leave." *Social Science Research* 40:1611–22.

Kremer, Monique. 2006. "Consumers in Charge of Care: The Dutch Personal Budget and its Impact on the Market, Professionals, and the Family." *European Societies* 8:385–401.

Krugman, Paul. 2005. "French Family Values." *New York Times,* July 29, 1. www .nytimes.com/2005/07/29/opinion/29krugman.html.

Kulik, Liat. 2011. "Developments in Spousal Power Relations: Are We Moving Toward Equality?" *Marriage & Family Review* 47:419–35.

Kumagai, Fumie. 1984. "The Life Cycle of the Japanese Family." *Journal of Marriage and the Family* 46:191–204.

Kunin, Madeline. 2012. *The New Feminist Agenda: Defining the Next Revolution for Women, Work, and Family.* White River Junction, VT: Chelsea Green.

Lakoff, George and Mark Johnson. 1980. *Metaphors We Live By.* Chicago: University of Chicago Press.

Lambert, Alysa, Janet Marler, and Hal Gueutal. 2008. "Individual Differences: Factors Affecting Employee Utilization of Flexible Work Arrangements." *Journal of Vocational Behavior* 73:107–17.

Lambert, Susan. 2009. "Making a Difference for Hourly Employees." Pp. 169–96 in *Work-Life Policies That Make a Real Difference for Individuals, Families, and Organizations,* edited by A. Crouter and A. Booth. Washington, D.C.: Urban Institute Press.

Lasch, Christopher. 1995. *Haven in a Heartless World: The Family Besieged.* New York: Norton.

Lee, Kristin Schultz. 2010. "Gender, Care Work, and the Complexity of Family Membership in Japan." *Gender and Society* 24:647–71.

Lino, Mark. 2012. "Expenditures on Children by Families, 2011." U.S. Department of Agriculture, Center for Nutrition Policy and Promotion. Miscellaneous Publication No. 1528-2011.

Luscher, Kurt. 2002. "Intergenerational Ambivalence: Further Steps in Theory and Research." *Journal of Marriage and Family* 64:585–93.

MacMillan, Ross. 2005. "The Structure of the Life Course: Classic Issues and Current Controversies." Pp. 3–24 in *The Structure of the Life Course: Standardized? Individualized? Differentiated? Advances in Life Course Research,* vol. 9. New York: Elsevier.

Mandel, Hadas. 2009. "Configurations of Gender Inequality: The Consequences of Ideology and Public Policy." *British Journal of Sociology* 60:693–719.

———. 2011. "Rethinking the Paradox: Tradeoffs in Work-Family Policy and Patterns of Gender Inequality." *Community, Work & Family* 14:159–77.

Mandel, Hadas and Moshe Semyonov. 2006. "A Welfare State Paradox: State Interventions and Women's Employment Opportunities in 22 Countries." *American Journal of Sociology* 111:1910–49.

Marks, Stephen R. 2006. "Understanding the Diversity of Families in the 21st Century and Its Impact on the Work Family Area of Study." Pp. 41–72 in *The Work-Family Handbook: Multidisciplinary Perspectives, Methods and Approaches*, edited by M. Pitt-Catsouphes, E. E. Kossek, and S. Sweet. Mahwah, NJ: Lawrence Erlbaum.

Marshall, Gordon. 2003. *A Dictionary of Sociology in Politics and Social Sciences*. New York: Oxford.

Matthews, T. J. and Brady Hamilton. 2009. "Delayed Childbearing: More Women Are Having First Child Later in Life," edited by U.S Department of Health and Human Services.

Matz-Costa, Christina and Marcie Pitt-Catsouphes. 2010. "Workplace Flexibility as an Organizational Response to the Aging of the Workforce: A Comparison of Nonprofit and For-Profit Organizations." *Journal of Social Service Research* 36:68–80.

McNeil, L. and M. Sher. 1999. "Dual-Science-CareerCouples." http://physics.wm .edu/~sher/survey.pdf.

Meiksins, Peter. 1998. "The Time Bind." *Monthly Review* 49:1–13.

Merton, Robert. 1968. *Social Theory and Social Structure*. New York: The Free Press.

Meyer, John and Brian Rowan. 1977. "Institutional Organizations: Formal Structure as Myth and Ceremony." *American Journal of Sociology* 83:340–63.

Milanovic, Branko. 2005. *Worlds Apart: Measuring International and Global Inequality*. Princeton, NJ: Princeton University Press.

Milliken, Frances, Jane Dutton, and Janice Beyer. 2002. "Understanding Organizational Adaptation to Change: The Case of Work-Family Issues." *Human Resource Planning* 13:91–107.

Misra, Joya. 2007. "Carework." *Blackwell Encyclopedia of Sociology*, edited by G. Ritzer. New York: Blackwell. www.sociologyencyclopedia.com/public.

Moen, Phyllis. 2008. "Not So Big Jobs and Retirements: What Workers (and Retirees) Really Want." *Generations* 31:31–36.

Moen, Phyllis, Erin Kelly, and Rachelle Hill. 2011. "Does Enhancing Work-Time Control and Flexibility Reduce Turnover? A Naturally Occurring Experiement." *Social Problems* 58:69–98.

Moen, Phyllis and Patricia V. Roehling. 2005. *The Career Mystique*. Boulder, CO: Rowman & Littlefield.

Moen, Phyllis and Donna Spencer. 2006. "Converging Divergences in Age, Gender, Health, and Well-Being: Strategic Selection in the Third Age." Pp. 127–44 in *Handbook of Aging and the Social Sciences*, edited by R. Binstock and L. George. New York: Elsevier Academic Press.

Moen, Phyllis and Stephen Sweet. 2002. "Two Careers, One Employer: Couples Working for the Same Corporation." *Journal of Vocational Behavior* 61:466–83.

———. 2004. "From 'Work-Family' to 'Flexible Careers': A Life Course Reframing." *Community, Work & Family* 7:209–26.

Moen, Phyllis, Stephen Sweet, and Raymond Swisher. 2004. "Embedded Career Clocks: The Case of Retirement Planning." Pp. 237–68 in *Advances in Life Course Research*. New York: Elsevier/JAI Press.

Moen, Phyllis, Ronit Waismel-Manor, and Stephen Sweet. 2003. "Success." Pp.133–52 in *It's About Time: Couples and Careers*, edited by P. Moen. Ithaca, NY: Cornell University Press.

Mohanty, Chandra Talpade. 2003. *Feminism Without Borders: Decolonizing Theory, Practicing Solidarity*. Durham, NC: Duke University Press.

Moshavi, Dan and Marianne Koch. 2005. "The Adoption of Family-Friendly Practices in Family-Owned Firms." *Community, Work & Family* 8:237–49.

Murray, Charles. 1995. *Losing Ground: American Social Policy, 1950–1980*. New York: Basic Books.

Muse, Lori. 2011. "Flexibility Implementation to a Global Workforce: A Case Study of Merck and Company, Inc." *Community, Work & Family* 14:249–56.

Nakano Glenn, Eveyln. 2002. *Unequal Freedom: How Race and Gender Shaped American Citizenship and Labor*. Cambridge, MA: Harvard University Press.

Neal, Margaret and Leslie Hammer. 2006. *Working Couples Caring for Children and Aging Parents: Effects on Work and Well-Being*. Mahwah, NJ: Lawrence Erlbaum.

Nippert-Eng, Christine. 1996. *Home and Work*. Chicago: University of Chicago Press.

Nowicki, Carol. 2002. "Fair Labor Standards Act." *Sloan Work and Family Encyclopedia*. http://workfamily.sas.upenn.edu/wfrn-repo/object/h3pe33 en5d9zq4kp.

O'Brien, Kathleen. 2001. "Trends; Fighting Sleep on the Job? Join the Crowd." *New York Times,* February 7. www.nytimes.com/2001/02/07/jobs/trends-fighting-sleep-on-the-job-join-the-crowd.html.

Ollier-Malaterre, Ariane. 2009. "Organizational Work-Life Initiatives: Context Matters—France Compared to the UK and the US." *Community, Work & Family* 12:159–78.

Organisation for Economic Co-operation and Development. 2010. www.oecd.org/statistics.

Osnowitz, Debra. 2010. *Freelancing Expertise: Contract Professionals in the New Economy*. Ithaca, NY: ILR Press.

Paid Family Leave Coalition. 2001. "Bargaining Fact Sheet: Family Leave and Expanding the Family and Medical Leave Act." http://workfamily.sas.upenn.edu/glossary/f/family-leave-definitions.

Pavalko, Eliza and Brad Smith. 1999. "The Rhythm of Work: Health Effects of Women's Work Dynamics." *Social Forces* 77:1141–62.

Pavalko, Eliza and Shari Woodbury. 2000. "Social Roles as Process: Caregiving Careers and Women's Health." *Journal of Health and Social Behavior* 41: 91–105.

Peters, Pascale, Laura den Dulk, and Tanja van der Lippe. 2009. "The Effects of Time-Spacial Flexibility and New Working Conditions on Employees' Work-Life Balance: The Dutch Case." *Community, Work & Family* 12:279–97.

Pfau-Effinger, Birgit. 2004. *Development of Culture, Welfare States and Women's Employment in Europe*. Burlington, VT: Ashgate.

Pfau-Effinger, Birgit and Maike Smidt. 2011. "Differences in Women's Employment Patterns and Family Policies: Eastern and Western Germany." *Community, Work & Family* 14:217–32.

Pfeffer, Jeffrey and Gerald R. Salancik. 1978. *The External Control of Organizations.* New York: Harper & Row.

Piore, Michael. 1977. "The Dual Labor Market and its Implications." Pp. 91–95 in *Problems in Political Economy,* edited by D. Gordon. Lexington, MA: D.C. Heath.

Pixley, Joy. 2008a. "Life Course Patterns of Career-Priorizing Decisions and Occupational Attainment in Dual-Earner Couples." *Work and Occupations* 35:127–63.

———. 2008b. "Career Prioritization in Dual-Earner Couples." *Work and Family Encyclopedia.* http://wfnetwork.bc.edu/encyclopedia_entry.php?id=6473&area=All.

Poster, Winifred and Srirupa Prasad. 2005. "Work-Family Relations in Transnational Perspective: A View from High-Tech Firms in India and the United States." *Social Problems* 52:122–46.

Presser, Harriet B. 2000. "Nonstandard Work Schedules and Marital Instability." *Journal of Marriage and the Family* 62:93–110.

———. 2003a. *Working in a 24/7 Economy: Challenges for American Families.* New York: Russel Sage Foundation.

———. 2003b. "Race-Ethnic and Gender Differences in Nonstandard Work Shifts." *Work and Occupations* 30:412–39.

Preston, Julia. 2008. "270 Illegal Immigrants Sent to Prison in Federal Push." *New York Times,* May 24. www.nytimes.com/2008/05/24/us/24immig.html?pagewanted=all.

Pugh, Allison. 2009. *Longing and Belonging: Parents, Children, and Consumer Culture.* Los Angeles: University of California Press.

Raich, Kathleen and Wendy Loretto. 2009. "Identity Work and the 'Unemployed' Worker: Age, Disability and the Lived Experience of the Older Unemployed." *Work, Employment and Society* 23:102–19.

Rhodes, Angel. 2002. "Long-Distance Relationships in Dual-Career Commuter Couples: A Review of Counseling Issues." *The Family Journal: Counseling and Therapy for Couples and Families* 10:398–404.

Richman, Amy, Janet Civian, Laurie Shannon, Jeffrey Hill, and Robert Brennan. 2008. "The Relationship of Pereived Flexibility, Supportive Work-Life Policies, and Use of Formal Flexible Arrangements and Occasional Flexibility to Employee Engagement and Expected Retention." *Community, Work & Family* 11:183–97.

Risman, Barbara J. 1998. *Gender Vertigo: American Families in Transition.* New Haven, CT: Yale University Press.

Roehling, Patricia V., Phyllis Moen, and Rosemary Batt. 2003. "Spillover." Pp. 101–21 in *It's About Time: Couples and Careers,* edited by P. Moen. Ithaca, NY: Cornell University Press.

Rybczynski, Witold. 1991. *Waiting for the Weekend.* New York: Viking.

Santorum, Rick. 2006. *It Takes a Family: Conservatism and the Common Good.* New York: Intercollegiate Studies Institute.

Schiebinger, Londa, Andrea Davies Henderson, and Shannon Gilmartin. 2008. *Dual-Career Academic Couples: What Universities Need to Know.* Stanford, CA: Stanford University Press.

Sennett, Richard. 1998. *The Corrosion of Character: The Personal Consequences of Work in the New Capitalism.* New York: W.W. Norton.

Smith, Dorothy E. 1993. "The Standard North American Family: SNAF as an Ideological Code." *Journal of Family Issues* 14:50–65.

Smith, Vicki. 2002. *Crossing the Great Divide: Worker Risk and Opportunity in the New Economy.* Ithaca, NY: Cornell University Press.

Smithson, Janet. 2006. "Using Focus Groups to Study Work and Family." Pp. 435–50 in *The Work and Family Handbook: Multidisciplinary Perspectives, Methods and Approaches*, edited by M. Pitt-Catsouphes, E. E. Kossek, and S. Sweet. Mahwah, NJ: Lawrence Erlbaum.

Soma, Naoko and Junko Yamashita. 2011. "Child Care and Elder Care Regimes in Japan." *Journal of Comparative Social Welfare* 27:133–42.

Sonnentag, Sabine. 2003. "Recovery, Work Engagement, and Proactive Behavior: A New Look at the Interface Between Nonwork and Work." *Journal of Applied Psychology* 88:518–28.

Stack, Carol B. 1997 [1974]. *All Our Kin: Strategies for Survival in a Black Community.* New York: Basic Books.

Statistics Bureau of Japan. 2012. "Statistical Handbook of Japan," edited by Statistics Bureau of Japan. Tokyo B. o. Japan.

Stevens, Daphne Pedersen, Krista Lynn Minnotte, Susan Mannon, and Gary Kiger. 2007. "Examining the 'Neglected Side of the Work-Family Interface': Antecedents of Positive and Negative Family-to-Work Spillover." *Journal of Family Issues* 28:242–62.

Still, Mary and Joan Williams. 2006. "A Legal Perspective on Family Issues at Work." Pp. 309–26 in *The Work and Family Handbook: Multi-Disciplinary Perspectives and Approaches*, edited by M. Pitt-Catsouphes, E. E. Kossek, and S. Sweet. Mahwah, NJ: Lawrence Erlbaum.

Stone, Pamela. 2007. *Opting Out? Why Women Really Quit Careers and Head Home.* Los Angeles: University of California Press.

Stuart, Mary and Eigil Boll Hansen. 2006. "Danish Home Care Policy and the Family: Implications for the United States." *Journal of Aging and Social Policy* 18:27–42.

Swanberg, Jenner, Marcie Pitt-Catsouphes, and Krista Drescher-Burke. 2005. "A Question of Justice: Disparities in Employees' Access to Flexible Schedule Arrangements." *Journal of Family Issues* 26:866–95.

Sweet, Stephen. 2011. "Anticipated and Unanticipated Consequences of Work-Family Policy: Insights from International Comparative Analyses." *Community, Work & Family* 14:117–18.

Sweet, Stephen and Mary Joggerst. 2008. "The Interlocking Careers of Older Workers and Their Adult Children." Boston: Boston Center on Aging and Work.

Sweet, Stephen, Christina Matz-Costa, Natalia Sarkesian, and Marcie Pitt-Catsouphes. Under Review. "Are Women Less Invested in Their Work? Explaining Gender Differences in Career Centrality."

———. 2013. *Changing Contours of Work: Jobs and Opportunities in the New Economy 2nd Edition.* Thousand Oaks, CA: Pine Forge Press.

———. 2012. "Gender Differences in Career Centrality: Explaining Variation in Industry and National Contexts." Gender, Work and Organization Conference, June 28, 2012, Keele University, Staffordshire, UK.

Sweet, Stephen and Phyllis Moen. 2004. "Intimate Academics: Coworking Couples in Two Universities." *Innovative Higher Education* 28:252–74.

———. 2006. "Advancing a Career Focus on Work and Family: Insights from the Life Course Perspective." Pp. 189–208 in *The Work and Family Handbook: Multi-Disciplinary Perspectives, Methods and Approaches,* edited by M. Pitt-Catsouphes, E. E. Kossek, and S. Sweet. Mahwah, NJ: Lawrence Erlbaum.

———. 2007. "Integrating Educational Careers in Work and Family: Women's Return to School and Family Life Quality." *Community, Work & Family* 10:233–52.

———. 2011. "Dual Earners Preparing for Job Loss: Agency, Linked Lives and Resilience." *Work and Occupations* 20:1–36.

Sweet, Stephen, Phyllis Moen, and Peter Meiksins. 2007. "Dual Earners in Double Jeopardy: Preparing for Job Loss in the New Risk Economy." Pp. 437–61 in *Workplace Temporalities,* vol. 17, *Research in the Sociology of Work,* edited by B. Rubin. New York: Elsevier.

Sweet, Stephen, Raymond Swisher, and Phyllis Moen. 2005. "Selecting and Assessing the Family-Friendly Community: Adaptive Strategies of Middle Class Dual-Earner Couples." *Family Relations* 54:596–606.

Swisher, Raymond, Stephen A. Sweet, and Phyllis Moen. 2004. "The Family-Friendly Community and Its Life Course Fit for Dual-Earner Couples." *Journal of Marriage and Family* 66:281–92.

Thevenon, Olivier and Anne Guthier. 2011. "Family Policies in Developed Countries: A 'Fertility Booster' with Side Effects." *Community, Work & Family* 14:197–216.

Thompson, E. P. 1967. "Time, Work-Discipline, and Industrial Capitalism." *Past and Present* 38:56–97.

Trefalt, Spela. 2010. "Interpersonal Aspects of Justice in Workplace Flexibility." In *Work and Family Encyclopedia.* http://wfnetwork.bc.edu/encyclopedia_entry .php?id=16766&area=All. Sloan Work and Family Research Network.

Ulrich, Laurel. 1982. *Good Wives: Image and Reality in the Lives of Women in Northern New England 1650–1750.* New York: Oxford University Press.

UNICEF. 2007. "Child Poverty in Perspective: An Overview of Child Well-Being in Rich Countries." United Nations Children's Fund, Florence, Italy.

United Nations. 2011. *Statistics and Indicators on Women and Men.* http://unstats .un.org/unsd/demographic/products/indwm.

U.S. Bureau of Labor Statistics. 2010. "A Profile of the Working Poor, 2008," edited by U.S. Dept. of Labor. Washington D.C.

U.S. Census. 2011. *The 2011 Statistical Abstract.* www.census.gov/compendia/statab/2011/2011edition.html.

U.S. Census. 2012. *The 2012 statistical abstract.* www.census.gov/compendia/statab.

U.S. Department of Labor. 2012. "Wage and Hour Division Family Medical Leave Act." www.dol.gov/whd/fmla.

Wadsworth, Lori. 2009. "Compressed Workweek Schedules." *Sloan Work and Family Encyclopedia.* http://workfamily.sas.upenn.edu/wfrn-repo/object/rz3n1a87f29m9d6u.

Warren, Elizabeth and Amelia Warren Tyagi. 2003. *The Two-Income Trap: Why Middle-Class Mothers and Fathers Are Going Broke.* New York: Basic Books.

Westman, Mina. 2005. "Crossover of Stress and Strain Between Spouses." *Work and Family Encyclopedia.* http://workfamily.sas.upenn.edu/wfrn-repo/object/lh6ru90gc27io7tf.

Wharton, Amy, Sarah Chivers, and Mary Blair-Loy. 2008. "Use of Formal and Informal Work-Family Policies on the Digital Assembly Line." *Work and Occupations* 36:327–50.

Williams, Joan. 2000. *Unbending Gender: Why Family and Work Conflict and What to Do About It.* New York: Oxford University Press.

———. 2007. "Legal Professions and Job Demands: Implications for Work/Life Balance." *Sloan Work-Family Encyclopedia.* http://workfamily.sas.upenn.edu/wfrn-repo/object/ps3xp23bf1p07d8x.

Wilson, William Julius. 1987. *The Truly Disadvantaged: The Inner City, the Underclass, and Public Policy.* Chicago: University of Chicago Press.

Wood, Stephen, Lilian de Menezes, and Ana Lasaosa. 2003. "Family-Friendly Management in Great Britain: Testing Various Perspectives." *Industrial Relations* 42:221–50.

World Bank. 2012. *World Development Indicators.* www.google.com/publicdata/explore?ds=d5bncppjof8f9.

World Health Organization. 2010. "The World Health Report." Geneva, Switzerland.

Zontini, Elisabetta. 2007. "Transnational Families." *Sloan Work and Family Encyclopedia.* http://workfamily.sas.upenn.edu/wfrn-repo/object/be4md-40po6iq2g3x.

Index

About the Author

Stephen Sweet is an associate professor of sociology at Ithaca College and visiting scholar at the Sloan Center on Aging & Work at Boston College. His books include *Changing Contours of Work* (2013, 2008), *Work and Family Policy: International Comparative Perspectives* (2012), *The Work and Family Handbook: Interdisciplinary Perspectives, Methods, and Approaches* (2005), *Teaching Work and Family: Strategies, Activities, and Syllabi* (2006), *College and Society: An Introduction to the Sociological Imagination* (2001), and *Data Analysis with SPSS: A First Course in Applied Statistics* (2011, 2008, 2003, 1998). He served as coeditor of the *Work and Family Encyclopedia* (2007–2010), and his studies on work, family, community, and inequality appear in a variety of publications, including *Work and Occupations, Women's Studies Quarterly, Generations, Research in the Sociology of Work, Sex Roles, Family Relations, New Directions in Life Course Research, Journal of Vocational Behavior, Journal of Marriage and the Family, Innovative Higher Education, Journal of College Student Development, Community, Work, and Family, Popular Music and Society*, and *International Journal of Mass Emergencies and Disasters*. His articles on teaching and curriculum development have been published in *Teaching Sociology, Critical Pedagogy in the Classroom*, and *Excellent Teaching in the Excellent University*. In addition to his research and teaching responsibilities, he serves as the director of the Sloan Early Career Work and Family Scholars Program. His current research focuses on issues relating to implementation of flexible work arrangements and the factors that shape dentification with work.

⑤SAGE research**methods**

The essential online tool for researchers from the
world's leading methods publisher

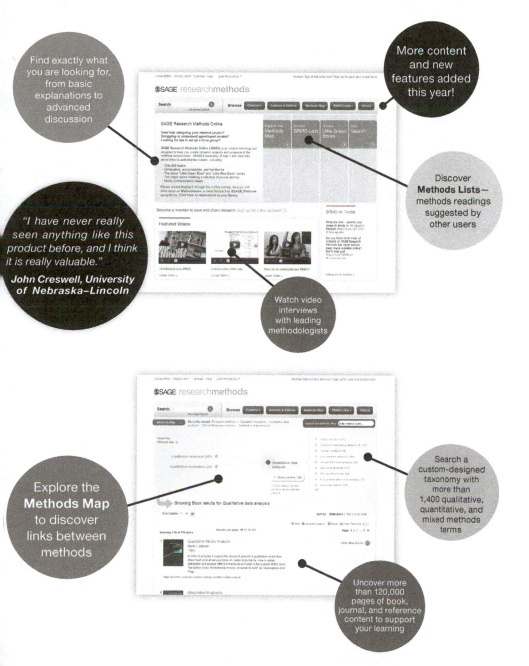

Find exactly what
you are looking for,
from basic
explanations to
advanced
discussion

More content
and new
features added
this year!

Discover
Methods Lists—
methods readings
suggested by
other users

*"I have never really
seen anything like this
product before, and I think
it is really valuable."*
**John Creswell, University
of Nebraska–Lincoln**

Watch video
interviews
with leading
methodologists

Search a
custom-designed
taxonomy with
more than
1,400 qualitative,
quantitative, and
mixed methods
terms

Explore the
Methods Map
to discover
links between
methods

Uncover more
than 120,000
pages of book,
journal, and reference
content to support
your learning

Find out more at
www.sageresearchmethods.com